Spelling Strategies (
The essential how to :

Thanks to all lovers of spelling, and my students.
Special thanks to Maria Parada, Annette Watson, H K Cutlip
and Darren Johnson for their kind words, encouragement
and dedication to their learning.

Joanne Rudling
www.howtospell.co.uk

Spelling for adults
It's never too late to improve your spelling

Spelling Strategies & Secrets:
The essential how to spell guide
by Joanne Rudling

© 2016 Joanne Rudling

ISBN: 978-0-9931931-4-9

Published by
How to Spell Publishing

Table of Contents

Introduction.. 4

The Most Common Misspelled Words List....................... 8

The Secrets of Spelling 16

Myth Busting.. 16

Handwriting.. 21

Dictionaries.. 22

The Do's and Don'ts of Spelling............................... 23

Glossary of Terms 25

Spelling Systems.. 26

Dyslexia Help 30

Spelling pep talk – making mistakes is good 31

Spelling Strategies – the tricks of spelling.............. 34

Words within Words.. 36

Troublesome Letters 50

Consonants... 50

Spotting Vowels 61

Silent Letters.. 66

Sound-Alikes – Homophones...................................... 78

Common homophones list... 94

Visual Spelling Patterns.. 104

Identifying Letter Patterns 105

Word Families.. 142

Building Words With Prefixes and Suffixes................... 156

Prefixes.. 158

Suffixes 167

Syllable Breakdown 182

Phonic Spelling Strategies..186
   Patterns, rhymes, sounds and rules 186
   Spelling vs. Pronunciation.. 207
Look, Say, Cover, Write, Check method................................ 214
Take an Interest in Words 216
American vs. British Spelling.. 220
Key Spelling Rules.. 230
Job Application Words... 240
Your Spelling Stories.. 249
Book & Website Recommendations...................................... 256
About the Author 258

Introduction

The purpose of *Spelling Strategies & Secrets* is to not only help you improve your spelling but also to increase your spelling knowledge, so that you understand why it is the way it is. It will help you see the regularities and patterns and eventually help you enjoy its strange, quirky ways, so you can remember spellings and have the confidence to write and express yourself the way you want to.

We have so many "tricky" spellings in English that we sometimes need help spelling them, or help with remembering certain letters. We might not need these words all the time, but when we do, we want to be able to spell them quickly, correctly, and without panicking and going for another word that we can spell but doesn't express exactly how we feel.

We're going to look at various strategies, such as using memory tricks (mnemonics); seeing words within words; knowing the history of words and silent letters; using syllable breakdown; understanding how words are built with prefixes and suffixes; sounding words out and rhyming words; identifying word families and letter patterns; and learning some spelling rules. Using different spelling strategies to help remember spellings is the aim. You might even use different strategies on one word.

We'll see concepts and words repeated so it reinforces learning, because it might take a few goes at getting these strategies and memory tricks into your brain.

It's vital to be able to write and express ourselves to friends and colleagues through emails and social media, and we shouldn't be excluded from this because of our spelling.

> Those who are not good at spelling often feel embarrassed about their lack of skill, and are unhappy about allowing others to see what they have written. They may even be reluctant to write at all. Sue Abell: *Helping Adults to Spell*

The aim of this book is to give you the confidence to spell well; to know that you can use these strategies to help you spell tricky words, and know that it's not "cheating". We have so many variations of spelling and a huge vocabulary that we need little reminders to spell some words. Even great spellers use them.

This book is not about learning obscure words but about learning common, everyday words that are some of the most misspelled in British (BrE) and American English (AmE).

It's important you learn the words that you need for your life, work, education, leisure, and job. Use a notebook to log these, especially the words you have problems with, and look at how you can use these strategies to help you remember how to spell them.

Ready for the journey?

**Enjoy spelling, enjoy writing,
and enjoy expressing yourself clearly.**

My Story (see *Your Spelling Stories* at the back)

I've been a lecturer and teacher trainer in literacy, writing, English, and ESOL for twenty years. I use and love all the strategies in this book, and have done so ever since I first learnt all about them when I started my literacy teacher training.

But before I became a teacher, I was interested in acting and scriptwriting. While taking a degree in TV and Film Scriptwriting, at age thirty, I realized I had problems with my spelling, especially homophones (they're, their, there; to, too; it's, its, etc.), and grammar problems (I'd/I'll, etc.). Punctuation was a nightmare too. Lecturers kept correcting all these problems. For years before this, I had rejections for my writing, maybe because of these. But still, I didn't do anything apart from try and be aware of some of my common mistakes, without really knowing how to remember which homophone was which, what grammar was, and where the hell you put apostrophes!

Anyway, one day in 1996, I was walking past Bournemouth Adult Education Centre and something inside told me to go in and offer to do some voluntary work, helping with reading and writing. So I did, and my teaching journey began. During an induction session, I heard about spelling strategies for adults and I was so excited, and also gobsmacked that I was never taught these.

And now, twenty years later, I have my own website, www.howtospell.co.uk, that helps thousands of adults throughout the world gain confidence in their spelling, and this includes both British and American English users.

If I can improve my spelling, you can too. All it takes is a big dose of determination, a bit of hard work, a keen eye to notice the rules and patterns everywhere, and lots of writing and using the spellings that are important in your life and work.

Style Notes

-ize and *-ise (realise/realize)* are both correct in British English, but American English only uses *-ize*. I use *-ize* throughout this book because *-ize* is the preferred house style of the *Oxford Dictionary*. My advice is to use one style and stick with it within a piece of writing.

If there are British (BrE) and American (AmE) spelling differences, then I write them side by side. It's always good to know the differences because it stops you getting confused when a red squiggly line appears under a word on the computer.

There are also some punctuation differences, too, with an Oxford comma, and punctuation inside the speech marks, but I won't go into these here (see my *Punctuation Guide*).

*learnt/learn**ed**, spelt/spelled, burnt/burned, spoilt/spoiled, misspelt/misspelled, smelt/smelled, spilt/spilled*

I first learnt all this in 1996. British (BrE)
I first learned all this in 1996. American (AmE)

BrE uses both endings, but AmE only uses the –ed ending.

David Crystal says: We hardly ever see the –t verb ending in American English, other than *dwelt* and *knelt*.

Do you feel that one of these sentences is more natural?
The forest burned for a week.
The forest burnt for a week.

It's quite common to choose the first because it gives a sense that the fire lasted for some time. We're more likely to use *burnt* for an event which is sudden and short and happened once, like *I burnt the toast* but sometimes the context is obscure, so we can use both endings.

The Most Common Misspelled Words List

Below are the most commonly misspelled words according to the *Oxford English Dictionary* and *Oxford English Corpus*. The tricky bits of the word, which most people make mistakes with, are beside the word in brackets/parentheses (AmE).

> *According to the Oxford Dictionary, not everyone spells these words wrong - but lots of people do! From sneaky silent letters to devious double letters, English sure doesn't make spelling easy.*
> Thanks to blog.oxforddictionaries.com

> Can you spell these words? Do you use any strategies to help you?
>
> What are the words and bits you find tricky? We'll see some of these again in the book, and many other words too.

accommodation (two c's, two m's) page 54

accessory/accessories (two c's, two s's) page 51, 148, 233

achieve/achieving/achievements (i before e) page 39, 63, 106, 135, 169, 232, 243

apparently (-ent) page 39, 56, 231

appearance (-ance) page 56, 133

argument (-gum-) page 39, 135, 233 / arguing (drop the 'e') page 232

basically (-ally) page 231

beginning/beginner (double n) page 234, 245

because (-au) page 39, 45, 46, 50, 58, 106, 118

beech/beach   beech – 61, 194, 195 / beach - 61, 124, 193, 194, 195, 235

believe/believable/unbelievable (i before e) page 36, 37, 45, 46, 63, 106, 157, 181, 190, 232

8

beautiful (-eau-) page 118, 124, 167, 170, 171, 175, 178, 179, 231, 233

business (busi) page 39, 66, 171, 172, 209, 233, 235

calendar (-dar) page 39, 61, 91

Caribbean (one r, double b) page 53

cemetery (three e's) page 61, 62, 147

changeable (keep the 'e') page 232, 238, 239

colleague (-ea- in the middle) page 244

coming (one m) page 232

committee (double m, double t, double e) page 55, 234, 244

completely (ends in -ely) page 56, 231

conscious page 150, 165 /conscience (-sc- in the middle) page 40

different/difference (double f, -ent/-ence) page 40, 131, 134, 135, 176, 209

difficult/difficulty (double f) page 40, 182, 192

definite/definitely (-ite) page 40, 61, 200, 231

dilemma (two m's) page 35, 36, 37, 38, 55

disappear (one s, two p's) page 56

disappoint (one s, two p's) page 56, 135, 180, 181

disapprove/disapproval (one s, two p's) page 56

discipline (notice all those i's) page 62

ecstasy (ecs- ends with -sy) page 57

ecstatic (ecs-) page 40, 57, 231

embarrass/embarrassing (two r's, two s's) page 50, 52, 135, 169

environment (n before m) page 40, 45, 46, 135, 244

equipment page 135, 169, 234

existence (ends in -ence) page 62

exhilarate (-arat) page 128

familiar (ends in -iar) page 41, 91, 245

finally (two l's) page 231, 238, 239

fluorescent (begins with fluor-) page 51

foreign (e before i) page 63, 73, 163

foreseeable/unforeseeable (fore-) page 166, 232, 233

forty (no 'u' begins with for-) page 50

forward (no 'e' begins with for-) page 166, 246

friend (-ie-) page 18, 41, 45, 46, 53, 63, 175, 180, 181, 183

glamorous (-mor-) page 150, 235 glamour/glamor 222

government (n before m) page 40, 135, 169

guarantee (-an-) page 70, 74, 232

harass/harassment (one r, two s's) page 52, 135, 169

honorary (-nor-) page 235

humorous (-mor- in the middle) page 150, 235

idiosyncrasy (ends in -sy) page 57

immediately (ends in -ely) page 55, 57, 128, 231

incidentally (ends in -ally) page 232

independent (ends in -ent) page 41, 61, 62, 131, 134, 135

interrupt (two r's) page 143

irresistible (ends in -ible) page 61, 62, 159, 180, 181

knowledge (remember the d) page 28, 53, 66, 75, 83, 135, 157, 169, 232

liaise/liaison (triple vowels -iai-) page 58, 62, 243

millennium/millennial (double l, double n) page 53

minuscule (minu-) page 53

mischievous (-ie-) page 63, 150

misspell/misspelled/misspelt (double s) page 7, 159

necessary (one c, two s's) page 50, 51, 146, 158, 159, 171

noticeable (don't drop the 'e') page 232

occasion (two c's, one s) + occasionally page 51

occurred (two c's, two r's) page 53, 234

parliament (-ia-) page 42, 135

persistent (ends with -ent) page 41, 131, 134

piece/peace (homophone) page 36, 37, 63, 78, 80, 81

possession (2 x two s's) page 30

preferred/preferring (two r's) page 136, 234

pronunciation (-nun-) page 43, 44, 202

publicly (ends in -cly) page 231

questionnaire (double n) page 244

queue (-eue) page 62, 94, 188, 229

really (two l's) page 124, 231

receive (e before i) page 18, 53, 63, 106, 201

receipt (e before i) page 63, 68, 71, 216

recommend (one c and 2 m's) page 55

referred/referring (2 r's) page 234, 243

remember (-mem- in middle) page 42, 62, 149

restaurant (-au-) page 118, 130, 131, 132

rhythm (h's and only one vowel 'y' as a vowel) / rhyme page 58

separate (-par- in middle) page 36, 37, 38, 61, 62, 128, 233

successful (two c's, two s's) page 170, 242

tendency (ends with -ency) page 30, 62

therefore (ends with -fore) page 166

tomorrow (one m, two r's) page 108, 245

truly (no e) page 53, 231, 233

weird (e before i) page 62, 63

wherever (one e in middle) page 235

Notes
If you don't want to write in this book, then
grab a notebook and write, draw, scribble your thoughts,
feelings, memory tricks, and the words you want to learn.

Self-Assessment Exercise 1

Which is correct? **Warning** – seeing a similar-looking spelling can really throw you, so that's why it's important to be able to use various spelling strategies to help you figure out which is which for this type of multiple choice exercise. But for now, use this as a self-assessment exercise.

1. a. weird   b. wierd

2. a. accommodate   b. accommdate

3. a. truely   b. truly

4. a. cemetary   b. cemetery

5. a. supercede   b. supersede

6. a. ecstacy   b. ecstasy

7. a. Caribbean   b. Carribean

8. a. harass   b. harrass

9. a. maintainence   b. maintenance

10. a. pronunciation   b. pronounciation

Self-Assessment Exercise 1. Answers

Did you use any strategies? Did you see what looked right? Did seeing the other spellings confuse you? We'll look at these words and how to remember them in the book.

1. a. weird ~~b. wierd~~

2. a. accommodate ~~b. accommdate~~

3. ~~a. truely~~ b. truly

4. ~~a. cemetary~~ b. cemetery

5. ~~a. supercede~~ b. supersede

6. ~~a. ecstacy~~ b. ecstasy

7. a. Caribbean ~~b. Carribean~~

8. a. harass ~~b. harrass~~

9. ~~a. maintainence~~ b. maintenance

10. a. pronunciation ~~b. pronounciation~~

Notes
What words do you need to work on?

Exercise 2. Which of these words is correct?
Remember, these type of exercises are only useful when
you can use your spelling strategies to help remember which
is which. Then again, you might be able to use your visual
memory to see what's right.

1. a. dilemma   b. dillemma   c. dillema

2. a. necessary   b. neccessary   c. necesary

3. a. miniscule   b. minusscule   c. minuscule

4. a. milennium   b. millennium   c. millenium

5. a. accesory   b. acessory   c. accessory

6. a. truely   b. truly   c. truley

7. a. tommorrow   b. tommorow   c. tomorrow

8. a. comittee   b. committee   d. committee

9. a. supercede   b. supersede   c. superceed

10. a. ocurred   b. occured   c. occurred

Exercise 2. Answers

1. a. dilemma ~~b. dillemma~~ ~~c. dillema~~
2. a. necessary ~~b. neccessary~~ ~~c. necesary~~
3. ~~a. miniscule~~ ~~b. minusscule~~ c. minuscule
4. ~~a. milennium~~ b. millennium ~~c. millenium~~
5. ~~a. accesory~~ ~~b. acessory~~ c. accessory
6. ~~a. truely~~ b. truly ~~c. truley~~
7. ~~a. tommorrow~~ ~~b. tommorow~~ c. tomorrow
8. ~~a. comittee~~ b. committee ~~d. committe~~
9. ~~a. supercede~~ b. supersede ~~c. superceed~~
10. ~~a. ocurred~~ ~~b. occured~~ c. occurred

Notes

15

The Secrets of Spelling

Myth busting

Secrets of spelling that shouldn't be secret!

Let's start off by looking at some important facts and bust some common myths about spelling.

Negative attitudes to spelling can create barriers to learning, which means they can stop you from learning how to spell well, stop you expressing yourself in writing, and can even stop you writing altogether.

Understanding all about spelling, why it is the way it is, and why we have some "strange" spellings will help you stop getting frustrated with it, and help you start loving and improving it.

Questions to get you thinking about spelling:

1. Does reading improve spelling?

2. Is English spelling totally irregular?

3. What's the percentage of words that have silent letters in them?

4. Why do we have silent letters?

5. Why don't we spell like we speak?

1. Reading vs. spelling

Reading is very important but it <u>won't</u> improve your spelling. Different skills are involved. Spelling is much more difficult than reading, so don't beat yourself up because you're a good reader but a rubbish speller. People from all walks of life, and even academics, can have spelling problems.

Look at, and say, the following words. They have the same long vowel sound 'e' + 's' but have 7 possible spellings.

      breeze, **knees**, th**ese**, fl**eas**, s**eize**, ch**eese**, t**ease**

Easy to read, not so easy to spell!

Thanks Basic Skills Agency.

So reading doesn't help spelling, but knowing all about spelling and how words are built with prefixes and suffixes, understanding rules, exceptions and their patterns, and identifying common letter patterns can help reading.

Spelling won't happen because we read, but improving spelling through reading means you have to consciously notice patterns and rules, and we don't do that when we read! A word must be consciously and deliberately learnt.

We skim over words when we read, whereas spelling is an active letter-by-letter activity.

Teachers assume that reading, once taught, automatically means that spelling will be "caught". But there is no correlation between reading ability and spelling ability. Spelling uses a set of active, productive, conscious processes that are not required for reading.
David Crystal: *The English Language*

Learners need spelling knowledge - gained by noticing how words and language behave. Remember that spellings are learned by focusing on the sound, look and feel of a word.
Basic Skills Agency, UK

According to Templeton & Bear, reading ability in children is ahead of their spelling ability. Many of them can read words like *shopping* and *bottle,* but spell them *shoping* and *botel.* This is true for adults too.

Do you know why *shopping* is spelled with a double 'p', and *bottle* with a double 't'? You'll discover why in the Spelling Rules, and the Phonic Spelling Strategies sections.

2. Is English spelling chaotic and totally irregular?

English spelling isn't chaotic, just complicated with strong reasons why it is the way it is. If you know these reasons, then you'll start to understand and respect spelling a lot more, even love it. We'll look at some of these reasons throughout the book.

English spelling is much more regular than we think. In fact, 75% of the time it's regular. But it's true that there are many irregular spellings; this is because it includes words borrowed from many languages, very old words, and silent letters.

David Crystal says that there seems to be both regularity and irregularity in English spelling. English spelling gives the impression of being more irregular than it really is. There are about 400 words in English whose spelling is wholly irregular – the trouble is, these are among the most frequently used words in the language.

Although among answer are aunt autumn blood build castle clerk climb colour comb come cough could course debt do does done dough eye friend gone great have hour island journey key lamb listen move none of once one only own people pretty quay receive rough said salt says shoe shoulder some sugar talk two was water were where who you

Notice a lot of these words have silent letters in them. Most silent letters used to be pronounced but are now silent because of changes in speaking but not spelling. Many silent letters show the history of the word and how it used to be pronounced centuries ago! They're the fossilized remains of a once spoken letter – little dinosaurs! But we love them for telling us the history of the word!

The English spelling system developed over the centuries, and the irregularities came about because of various writers trying to fit their alphabet and sounds to English. Latin writers, French scribes, the printing presses of the 1400s, and the 16th century academics all brought their own "strange" ways of spelling words.

Also, there was a dramatic change in pronunciation during the Great Vowel Shift between 1450 and 1750, when many vowel and consonant sounds changed or disappeared. Unfortunately, this happened when spelling had become fixed.

Pronunciation is always changing, but we don't alter spellings or we'd be forever changing them. And anyway, which pronunciation would we use as a benchmark for spelling? My northern accent, southern accents, American, Australian?

3. 60% of English words have silent letters in them
Silent letters can cause all sorts of problems spelling the word, or looking for the word in a dictionary. But if you know the history of why there are silent letters, it'll not only improve your spelling, but also stop you getting frustrated with it (more information in the Silent Letter section).

4. Why do we have silent letters?
As I mentioned, most silent letters used to be pronounced but then dropped out of fashion. Speaking and pronunciation is forever changing, but the spelling system doesn't reflect this. For example, knock, knee, knuckle, gnaw, gnat are all Viking/Old Norse words. The 'k' and 'g' used to be

pronounced then slowly dropped out of fashion, but were still left in the spelling.

Sometimes, the way something is spelled shows us the history of the word and the way people spoke it centuries ago - and that's why the spelling might seem a bit strange.

5. Why don't we spell like we speak?

To have a regular phonics "sounding out" system that works, there would have to be only one way of spelling each sound. This is true in some languages, but not English.

There have always been many different accents in English and to decide which accent, or dialect, to base the spelling on would be impossible, and always has been impossible.

English has never had an academy of English to oversee grammar, vocabulary and spelling. For centuries, people spelt how they wanted to. It was only in 1830 that a group of "gentlemen" decided to write the definitive dictionary of English spelling (later to become the Oxford Dictionary).

According to Pacquita Boston, these "gentlemen" weren't interested in making spelling simple, or linking it to pronunciation, or making English easy to read. Their task was to choose a spelling "they felt best reflected the history or origin of each word. They often had a great range of spellings to choose from. They unified spelling, but did not simplify it."

Good spellers often try and sound out an unfamiliar spelling to see if it sounds like a pattern they know. They then write it down to see if it looks right. Often, the spelling does reflect pronunciation and can give clues, or very clear indications, of likely spelling: *light, right, bright; thick, sick, lick, trick* (see the Phonics & Letter Pattern sections).

Handwriting

Always write and type in lower case (small letters) with capitals for proper nouns. It's easier to write in and means you can see the shape of the word: *education* Britain *brilliant* **words**

Writing or typing a lot trains your muscle memory to remember the shape, feel and flow of the word, and soon it'll seem like the spelling is writing itself.

Block capitals are ALL CAPITALS. Never write in block capitals unless it's on a form because it's hard to write in and hard to "see" the spelling.

As well as having a visual memory and an auditory memory, we also have a motor memory. This is to do with movement. Our muscles can "remember" shape and movement so that when we write a word, they will form and imprint of the flow and pattern of the letters.

Anne Betteridge: *Adult Learners' Guide to Spelling.*

Dictionaries

Knowing the meaning of words, as well as knowing how to use them are important strategies to learning a word or spelling.

Don't be afraid of looking in a dictionary to not only check the spelling, but also the meaning and how the word is used in context in a sentence. And for some online dictionaries, you can check the pronunciation too.

Put these on your favourites/favorites bar, or bookmark them, so you can access them all the time.

www.oxforddictionaries.com - British & American
www.macmillandictionary.com - British & American
http://dictionary.cambridge.org - British & American
www.merriam-webster.com - American online

According to David Crystal, *using dictionaries is important because spelling does not stand still. It changes with the times, as do features of language, such as vocabulary and grammar. A surprising number of words in a general dictionary vary in the way they can be written: is it moon or Moon, flowerpot or flower-pot, judgment or judgement?*

The Do's and Don'ts of Spelling

(do's and **don'ts** can also be spelt/spelled **dos** and **don'ts)**

Do learn about spelling - it's never ever too late to learn to spell. If you really want to spell well then learn the rules, the conventions, notice spelling patterns, letter patterns, and understand why spelling is the way it is.

Do write as often as you can. Also write in lowercase/small letters, with capitals in the right places for proper nouns, such as Joanne, Britain, Canada. This means you can see the shape of the word. Also use the capital I for I, I'm, I've, I'll, I'd.

Don't write in BLOCK CAPITALS unless it's on a form because it's hard to write in and to read.

Do use the words you like even if you're not sure of the spelling. Ask someone or try to use a dictionary, or spell checker.

Do try to find your own errors. Proofread your emails, comments, messages, and go over them again and again. Go over your writing slowly and read it out loud to see if you've missed any words, missed letters, or wrote the wrong word, especially homophones. Be careful with predictive text, it's convenient, but it might give you a weird, totally incorrect word.

Do make a correct copy of the words you need to learn for your life, work, training, education – make a little dictionary for yourself and use the Look Say Cover Write Check method (more details later).

Do practise (practice AmE) the words you want to use and test yourself regularly.

Don't look at or concentrate on the wrong spelling (remember, your visual memory is strong). Figure out what your mistakes are and then concentrate on the correct spelling and how to remember it.

Don't learn words you'll never use. Concentrate on those you need.

Don't try to learn too many words at once. Pick the most important keywords for your work, life and education.

Don't rely on the sound of the word for its spelling. Think about it in as many ways as you can – the look, meaning, sound, feel, emotions...

Do use memory tricks and spelling strategies.

Do enjoy spelling for all its quirky ways, and stay passionate about your learning and life.

As your knowledge of words increases, your confidence in learning improves, your ability to use a dictionary develops and your memory bank of words grow larger, you will start being able to predict likely spelling patterns or feel able to learn whole groups of words at once, and learning and remembering spellings will become easier for YOU.

Basic Skills Agency's *The Spelling Pack*

Glossary of Terms

These words are useful to know.

Nouns are things or people: *table, chair, London, Joanne...*
Singular nouns = *a dog, a watch, a chair, a bus pass...*
Plural nouns = *dogs, watches, chairs, bus passes...*
Proper nouns (with capital letter/s) = *Joanne, London, America, Bournemouth College, BBC, Harvard, Mrs Smith...*
A memory trick to remember what a noun is 'n' in <u>n</u>oun = <u>n</u>ame

Adjectives describe nouns: a <u>*blue*</u> bag, a *happy* baby, a *boring* life, *healthy* person, this is *easy*
Some adjectives have **-ing** and **-ed** suffix endings:
She's *excited*. This is *interesting*. It's not *boring*.

Verbs show action or being: to *work*, I *watched*, they *are*, *listen*, *read*, you're *learning* and *reading* this...
Third person means *he, she, it* and we add 's' or 'es' to regular verbs: *He sees, She runs, It moves, He watches, She wishes* (see Suffix section)

Prefixes and suffixes are little words we put on root words to change the meaning and grammar - **misunderstanding, immaturely**
prefixes = in-, un-, mis-, dis-, im-, il-, sub-, pre-...
suffixes = -ed, -ing, -tion, -able, -ible, -er, -or...
(More in the Building Words with Prefixes & Suffixes section.)

Syllable breakdown is about breaking a word down into little spoken chunks, and each chunk usually has a vowel in it
1 syllable: trick
2 syllables: paper – pa/per
3 syllables: computer – com/pu/ter
4 syllables: application – ap/pli/ca/tion
5 syllables: uncomfortable – un/com/for/ta/ble
(More in the Syllable Breakdown section.)

Spelling Systems

In this section, we're looki͞n
learning spelling from some ͞e
interests you.

A System for Spelling (thanks to th͞

Analyse	Plan

- What words do you have problems with?
- Highlight parts that cause problems.

- Keep a notebook of words that are important for you
- Revise spellings regularly

- Us͞ pell check and dictionaries

Use Spelling Strategies	**The System**	Use a Variety of Practice

Take an Interest in Words

Use various strategies for learning and remembering spellings
- Use Look Say Cover Write method
- Use memory tricks
- Identify letter patterns
- Know how to build words with prefixes & suffixes
- Use syllable breakdown
- Learn spelling rules and the exceptions

- Know why English spelling is the way it is through the history of spelling & the origins of words
- Love and have fun with words
- Know word families and how they're related by meaning & pattern

Engage with spelling in all sorts of ways – look, hear, say, touch, use, emotionally
- Do exercises, games, word searches
- Do spelling tests and dictations
- Make a letter pattern dictionary & write letter pattern stories
- Write and use the spellings in emails, comments, texts

Five Spelling Systems

Good spellers use all sorts of ways to learn and remember
spellings. In this section, we'll look at some of these in more
detail, but don't worry about the technical terms; just know
that these are suggestions about how we learn, or can learn
to spell, and how we can combine many of these "systems" to
help us.

According to Johanna Stirling, there are five useful
systems/ways of learning spelling:

1. Know the history of spelling (*Etymological System*). This is
about knowing the history of English spelling and why it is
the way it is. According to Johanna Stirling, this is one of
the most important ways to really learn and understand
English spelling because it explains why we have those
"strange" letter patterns like -ough, -igh, wh-, kn-, etc.

Knowing the history of English spelling will also help you feel
less frustrated and annoyed with spelling. We'll look at why
spelling is the way it is in the sections on Silent Letters,
Letter Patterns, Word Families and Taking an Interest in
Words.

2. Know how words are built (*Morphological System*). Think
about words morphing/changing when adding small words to a
root word! By adding prefixes and suffixes to root words,
you change the meaning - *uncomfortable*, *unhappy*,
dissatisfied, etc. We'll see this again in the Building Words
with Prefixes and Suffixes section.

According to Professor Larry Beason, understanding this
system can provide a more accurate understanding of our
spelling system, and studying it will improve spelling.

27

3. Seeing patterns and links (*Lexical System*). This is a very interesting system. It's about word families with the same letter pattern and related meaning (not the phonetic/sound link): *two, twice, twelve, between... sign, signal, signify, signpost... know, knowledge, knowledgeable...* We'll see this in the Word Families section.

4. Sounding out words (*Phonological System*). This is about using the sounds of words to help us spell. English is only about 45-50% phonetically regular, so it's tricky relying on phonics. But we tend to try and sound out words when we don't know how to spell a new/strange word, and we do this to hear if it relates to a spelling pattern we know. We then use our visual memory to see if it looks right. We'll see some useful strategies in the Phonetic Strategies section.

5. Seeing spelling patterns and rules (*Graphemic System*). This is about seeing letter patterns, understanding word endings and knowing some spelling rules. We'll see this in the sections on Visual Spelling Patterns, Suffixes, and Spelling Rules.

More interesting thoughts from some spelling experts.

There are five ways into a word:
1. Think about the meaning of the word.
2. Unpack the way the word is making that meaning by looking for the base word and prefixes and suffixes.
3. Find out where the word has come from.
4. Listen to the sounds in the word.
5. Check if any spelling rules apply.

Good spellers use all of these strategies. Poor spellers rely on sounds!

Misty Adoniou

Senior Lecturer in Language, Literacy at University of Canberra

English spelling must engage the eyes as well as an understanding of word meaning and spelling structure to help the brain register where and why letters appear in the patterns that they do.
Sally Raymond: Spelling Rules, Riddles and Remedies

Knowing the story behind why a word is spelled in a certain way helps kids [and adults] see that spelling isn't the illogical mess they think it is.
David Crystal

Increasingly, however, pupils also need to understand the role of **morphology** and **etymology**. National Curriculum for schools UK

Can you remember these from the Five Spelling Systems?

Notes	Thoughts and questions

Dyslexia Help

According to the lovely people at beatingdyslexia.com: "By remembering how words are spelt in more than one way will give you a stronger and more precise memory of them. This is called creating layers of memory."

Remembering with your eyes:
This is about using the visual appearance of words to remember how they are spelt: *tendency*

Remembering with your ears:
Pronouncing a word the way it is written is a classic spelling tip. Say it out loud, the way it is spelt, to make it stick in your mind:
iron "I ron"

Remembering with your brain:
This one is about how the English language works. Every rule in English was made to be broken. It's a better idea to look at the letter patterns: *joke – joking* (drop the 'e' with –ing rule)

Remembering with your imagination:
This is about using imagination and association to remember how words are spelt: *possession* the s's are guarding the 'e'

www.beatingdyslexia.com/spelling-tips.html

We'll see more from beatingdyslexia.com in the Spotting Vowels section.

Spelling pep talk – making mistakes is good

As adults, we feel so stupid when we make mistakes. We give ourselves a hard time about it, and even hate ourselves for it. And making spelling mistakes, or not knowing how something is spelt, is right up there.

According to a report by the NRDC on adult writing, spelling was identified as the "bit of writing" that's the most difficult.

Q2. Which bits of writing are difficult?
52 per cent said spelling was the most difficult
9.9 per cent punctuation
9.9 per cent grammar

(Kelly, Soundranayagam, Grief)

Spelling can be learned – it just takes a bit of time, effort, and thinking about the mistakes made, and understanding why spelling is the way it is.

Don't get stressed if you forget a spelling. If you learn something or see a spelling once, it doesn't mean you'll remember it. You have to keep working on the spelling to get it into your long-term memory. You'll probably have to keep working on the memory tricks you come up with too.

Remember, you need to keep practising/practicing (AmE) spelling and keep writing, which I'm sure you do with social media comments, and emails. So don't give yourself a hard time; instead, know that you're doing a little bit every day to improve your spelling.

Just because you have seen a word and copied it down once, does not mean it's yours. You won't "own" that word to use it when you want to without really **learning** it, **committing** it to memory in the first place.
Basic Skills Agency: Spelling Pack

Studying a word/spelling in a deliberate, active and conscious way means you need to notice the features of words. Pay attention to how words are made up of the letter patterns, root words, prefixes, suffixes and rules. Also, writing and spelling are linked, so write.

Remember that most forgetting happens in the first few hours so you need to:
- revise little and often;
- revise a newly learned word/memory trick within 20 seconds or so, and then review it again an hour later;
- get a good night's sleep, which helps memorization, so look at the word before bed, then again in the morning;
- not leave it more than a week before you revise the word;
- use the word in your writing, or take a real conscious note of it when you see the word in print, online, in ads.

If you divide your notes like this, it improves your memory retention

Notes	Thoughts and questions
	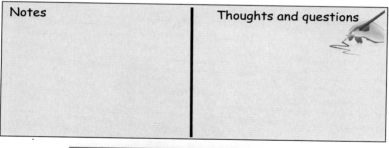

What good spellers have in common is they:
- use different strategies to remember spellings
- can see patterns and regularity in spelling
- are interested in words, their origins, meaning and spelling
- can see errors when proof-reading
- can break words into syllables/parts and spell those parts
- can hear new words and link them to letter patterns
- recognize letter patterns
- know spelling rules and exceptions
- have a strong visual memory, and can see a word in their mind and spell it

You must work at and study spelling - notice it, think about it, question it and take notes.

Taking notes, writing your thoughts, and questioning helps to boost your retention/remembering by 50%.

And, of course, you must write and use the spellings.

Enjoy. Have fun. Be inspired.

Spelling Strategies - the tricks of spelling

Do you use any "tricks" to help you remember a spelling?

Using spelling strategies/memory aids to remember how to spell difficult words is one of the most important aspects of spelling.

It's reassuring to know you can use a variety of spelling strategies to help you recall spellings, and in this book, we're going to look at strategies such as:

- Using memory tricks (mnemonics).
- Seeing a word within a word.
- Seeing vowels.
- Noticing prefixes and suffixes.
- Seeing letter patterns.
- Recognising word families linked by meaning.
- Using syllable breakdown.
- Spelling with rhymes, saying and acronyms.
- Understanding the history of spelling and why some words are spelled the way they are.
- Knowing spelling rules.

You might find some of these spelling strategies very useful and they work for you, and some you won't like or aren't useful – that's OK and normal. This is a chance to try, and learn, some of the best strategies to help your spelling.

Other people's memory tricks are useful to know and use, but if you invent your own it means the process of coming up with one will help fix it in your brain, and it's personal to you, so you'll remember it!

There are lots of different strategies and techniques to learn a spelling – some you might like and others you might not like - use whatever works, makes sense and is logical to you. You might use different strategies for the same word – that's OK.

When using memory tricks to remember a spelling:
- have fun;
- use humour/humor (AmE);
- be outrageous, rude, bawdy (you'll remember it then!);
- give the word an emotional attachment;
- draw or doodle a picture of the memory trick and word (this engages the brain to make strong memory links).

Mnemonics are memory aids/memory tricks to help you remember spellings. They could be a sentence, special word, sayings, a short poem, or rhyme. We're going to look at lots of these but you don't need to remember all of them, only the ones you need. If the memory trick doesn't work for you, make up one that does.

Don't worry about whether you'll forget these "strange" and very useful mnemonics - deep down in those brain cells, they're there! And something will trigger **Emma** and her di**lemma**, or the perman**ent** resid**ent** in the t**ent**, or the envel**opes** in stati**onery**.

Next, we're going to look at the word-within-word strategy, and use some of the techniques below (and throughout the book).

The storage and recall of spelling is all about hearing, seeing, writing, drawing, deep thinking, emotions. All these activities fire neurons in the brain:

1. Adopting the role of "spelling detective" actively promotes thinking and reasoning skills.

2. Using memory prompts captures interest and thought, but needs to be rehearsed and revised.

3. Drawing pictures engages the brain in developing strong memory traces [in the 'Note' sections, draw and doodle if the mood takes you].

4. Recall spelling through different activities.

Sally Raymond: *Spelling Rules, Riddles and Remedies*

Words within Words

Seeing words within words can help you remember the difficult bits of the word, the tricky letter patterns (-ie- or -ei-), the silent letters, double consonants, which homophone is which, and helps break down long words.

> Finding words within words is another strategy that helps memory of long spellings. The most useful is when we can find words with related meaning that help us to spell.
> Johanna Stirling: *Teaching Spelling*

> Many words have shorter words inside them. The English language is a difficult language when it comes to spelling, but one good thing about it is that it contains patterns of letters which are repeated again and again. This is why we can find so many words inside other words.
> Anne Betteridge: *Adult Learners' Guide to Spelling*

If you're a fan of howtospell.co.uk and my books, then you might have seen, or know, some of these mnemonics because I repeat them again and again, which is good because it helps get them into your long-term memory (and I love and use them too).

Can you see the word within the word in these tricky words?

1. *believe* – when you don't tell the truth
2. *piece* – you can eat this with a meat or fruit filling
3. *there* – place
4. *hear* – to listen with this
5. *separate* – an animal is in this word
6. *dilemma* – a girl's name

a. *believe* – lie
b. *piece* – pie
c. *there* – here
d. *hear* – ear
e. *separate* – rat
f. *dilemma* – Emma

When you use a word-within-a-word strategy:
1. See the word in the word.
2. Try and link the "hidden" word to a related saying. Coming up with your own unique saying/sentence will help make the spelling, and memory trick, memorable and gives you a clue to the word in the word. Be as crazy as you want.
3. Draw a picture. Find photos/pictures. Remember, drawing a picture engages the brain in developing strong memory links. Or visualize the picture it creates in your mind's eye.

believe (tricky bit: -ie-)
1. See the word within the word *be lie ve*
2. Make a sentence - *Never believe a lie*
   If you lie, I won't believe you.
   There's a lie in believe.
3. Draw a picture, or picture it.

piece (*peace* or *piece?*)
1. **Pie** in **pie**ce
2. *I'd like a piece of pie.*
3. Picture it!

there (*there, their, they're?*)
1. **Here** in **there**
2. *Here there where everywhere nowhere.*
3. Notice the **here** in all the "place" words in 2.

hear (*here or hear?*)
1. **Ear** in **hear**
2. *Hear with your **ear** and learn.*
3.

More on these homophones later.

separate (tricky bit: -arat-)
1. A **rat** in sep**arat**e
2. Separate a **rat**
   There's **a rat** in sep*a*rate. "sep a rat e"
   Pull **apart** to separate.
   Never separate a **para** from his parachute.

dilemma (tricky bit: double 'm')
1. See Emma in dil<u>emma</u>
2. ***Emma** is in a di**lemma**.*
3.

Key tricky words and their memory tricks

> Anything goes. Don't shy away from silly or sensational associations. You may even disagree with what your trick sentence says. If it works for you, don't reject it.
> *Demonic Mnemonics*

achieve/achievement (-ie-)
achieving (drop the 'e' with –ing)

Eve achieved the achievements she wanted.
The chief achieved everything.
Or use the old saying: "i before e except after c".

apparently (2 p's, 2 a's, rent)
apparent + ly = *apparently*   *ap/pa/rent/ly*
A posh parent can pay the rent.

argument (no 'e') drop the 'e' with 'ment'
argue + ment = argument
I lost an 'e' in an argument.
I always argue and always lose that 'e' in arguments.
Think of chewing gum when you chew over an argument.

bargain *When you get a bargain, you gain.*

because Can you see the **use** in because?
Use this trick because then you'll always understand.

bicycle *When it's icy, don't ride your bicycle.*

business (tricky bit: *busi*)
We say "biz ness"! Careful of the bus and silent 'i'
It's good business to go by bus.
Having a business is not a sin.

Spelling rule - change the 'y' to 'i' with 'ness'
busy + ness = *business*,   happy + ness = *happiness*

calendar *Check your calendar for dates and see if you can lend a hand.*

39

conscience con + science
Don't sil<u>ence</u> your cons<u>cience</u> about sc<u>ience</u>.

dangerous *Anger is dangerous.*

definite/definitely (tricky bit: the two i's)
Finite possibilities are definite.
Write it definite.
Definite has two i's in it.
de + finite + ly = definitely

different/difference (tricky bits: double f and -ent)
I beg to <u>differ</u> but the rent is <u>different</u> every year.
What's the <u>difference</u> if we <u>differ</u> in the end?

difficult / difficulty (double f)
difficult + y = difficulty
The two f's are doubly difficult.
See the cult in difficult - cults are difficult to fight for.

ecstatic – *My ever crazy hair static*
doesn't make me ecstatic.

excellent (tricky bit: double 'l' + ent)
Extra cells in your brain are excellent.
Can you see all the e's? e xc e ll e nt

environment and **government** (tricky bit: both have a silent 'n')
Can you see the words within these two words?

government = govern + ment

Can you see the **iron** in environment?
We can iron out the environment.
A new environment will iron it out.

familiar *That liar looks familiar.*

peculiar *He's a familiar peculiar liar.*
*These words are **peculiar** because they have **unfamiliar** patterns.*
They break down into syllables: fam/il/i/ar pe/cu/li/ar

forest *I best rest in the forest before I head west.*

friend *Is this the end, my friend?*
My friend has fries at the end of the week on Friday.
If you "fri" your friend, he'll come to an end.

hospital *You might have to spit in a hospital.*

insistent *My sis was insistent about the tent.*

instead *Drink tea instead of coffee.*

-ent letter pattern

independent *(See all those e's - in de pen dent)*
The independent voters didn't make a dent in the election.
The independent value of the pen depends on the dent in it.

present *He sent a present.*

permanent *The man is a permanent resident of the tent.*

persistent *My sis is so persistent about getting a tent.*

You can't dent the ego of a confident independent prudent student.

succulent *The cucumber he lent us was succulent.*

(More –ent words in the Letter Pattern section.)

hear *You hear with your **ear** and **learn.***
hear, heard, hearing

listen *Listen to the **list**.*

jealousy *Jealousy is **lousy**.*

measurement
*Be **sure** to measure your measurements.*

neurotic *They're **neuro**tic about leaving the **euro** zone.*

parliament *Liam went to the Houses of Parliament.*
or *I am parliament.*

secretary *A **secret**ary will keep **a secret**.*

significant *Sign if I cant (can't). Notice all those i's.*

sincerely since rely
*Since I **rely** on you, I **since**rely need you.*

soldier *Soldiers sometimes **die** in battle.*

suede *Sue loves **sue**de.*

teacher *The teacher teaches each student.*

their *He's **their** son and **heir**. It's **their** heirloom. The inheritance is **theirs** because they are **heirs**.*

together *to get her.*
*Let's go round **together to get her**.*

recovery *For a full re**cover**y, you need to **cover** it.*

remember re + member
Remember all those e's.

young *You are so **young**.*

42

Exercise

Can you see the word hidden in these words?

1. Connecticut - to join
2. comparison - capital city
3. sincerely - 5-letter word
4. prevalent - an alcoholic drink
5. pronunciation - in a religious order

Thanks to Murray Suid: *Demonic Mnemonics*

Exercise

Thanks to bbc.co.uk/skillswise

How many shorter words can you find in these words?

1. cardigan (4 words)
2. fortunate (4 words)
3. management (5 words)
4. transportable (6 words)

Exercise

Find the body parts. Each word has a body part but one word has two body parts.

alarm, diagnose, friendship, merchandise, obeyed, potatoes, searching, slippers

Thanks to Johanna Stirling's *Teaching Spelling*

Exercise Answers

Can you see the word hidden in these words?
Thanks to Murray Suid: *Demonic Mnemonics*

1. **Connect**icut - to join (connect)

2. com**paris**on - capital city (Paris)

3. **since**rely - 5-letter word (since)

4. prev**ale**nt - an alcoholic drink (ale)

5. pro**nun**ciation - in a religious order (nun)

Exercise Answers

1. cardigan – *car, card, dig, an*

2. fortunate – *for, fort, tuna, ate*

3. management – *man, age, manage, men, gem*

4. transportable – *ran, port, transport, tab, table, able*

Exercise Answers

Find the body parts. Each word has a body part but one word has two body parts.

a**larm**, diag**nose**, friend**ship**, merc**hand**ise, ob**eye**d, pota**toes**, s**ea**rching/sear**ching**, sl**ip**pers

Thanks to Johanna Stirling's *Teaching Spelling*

Exercise

Words within Words Exercise

Underline the "hidden" word and then write it out.

e.g. Underline an animal in edu<u>cat</u>ion   <u>cat</u>

1. Underline something that's not true in **believe** _____

2. Underline a past tense verb meaning end of life in **studied** _____

3. Underline a type of metal in **environment** _____

4. Underline the final part in **friend** _____

5. Underline a part of the head in **learn** _____

6. Underline a number in **money** _____

7. Underline another word for everything in **usually** _____

8. Underline another word for hello in **while** _____

9. Underline a three-letter verb in **because** _____

Thanks to Johanna Stirling's *Teaching Spelling*

Exercise Answers

Underline the "hidden" word and then write it out.

e.g. Underline an animal in edu<u>cat</u>ion   <u>cat</u>

1. Underline something that's not true in bel<u>ie</u>ve   <u>lie</u>

2. Underline a past tense verb meaning end of life in stu<u>died</u>   <u>died</u>

3. Underline a type of metal in envi<u>ron</u>ment   <u>iron</u>

4. Underline the final part in fri<u>end</u>   <u>end</u>

5. Underline a part of the head in l<u>ear</u>n   <u>ear</u>

6. Underline a number in m<u>one</u>y   <u>one</u>

7. Underline another word for everything in usu<u>all</u>y   <u>all</u>

8. Underline another word for hello in w<u>hi</u>le   <u>hi</u>

9. Underline a three-letter verb in beca<u>use</u>   <u>use</u>

Thanks to Johanna Stirling's *Teaching Spelling* book

46

Exercise Which is correct?
Use your visual memory or your knowledge of words
within words to help.

1. a. piece   b. peice

2. a. seperate   b. separate

3. a. because   b. becuase

4. a. friend   b. freind

5. a. envirament   b. environment

6. a. sincerly   b. sincerely

7. a. permunent   b. permanent

8. a. dilemma   b. dillema

9. a. persistent   b. persistant

10. a. Their son   b. They're son

11. a. Can you hear me?   b. Can you here me?

12. a. arguement   b. argument

13. a. acheivement   b. achievement

14. a. remember   b. remmember

Exercise Answers

1. a. piece   b. peice

2. a. seperate   b. separate

3. a. because   b. becuase

4. a. friend   b. freind

5. a. envirament   b. environment

6. a. sincerly   b. sincerely

7. a. permunent   b. permanent

8. a. dilemma   b. dillema

9. a. persistent   b. persistant

10. a. Their son   b. They're son

11. a. Can you hear me?   b. Can you here me?

12. a. arguement   b. argument

13. a. acheivement   b. achievement

14. a. remember   b. remmember

My words within words, memory tricks, notes, thoughts, doodles, drawings...

Troublesome Letters

Consonants

> Focusing on the specific letters of words that cause problems brings your awareness to the source of the mistake, and helps you to commit the proper spelling to memory. *esl.dictionary*

Most people usually know the beginning and endings of words, and understand the patterns (*-ation, -ary, -ness, -ing*), but it's the individual letters within a word that usually cause problems, especially single or double letters in words like *embarrass, necessary, accommodate.*

Link the word to a relevant saying or rhyme, with the tricky letters making up the saying, like in the word within words strategy. If you don't understand a memory trick I've used, then spend some time working it out – this will help you study the word and learn it. Better still, make up your own tricks – it's fun!

---

forty = 40

No 'u' in forty
Four, fourteen but u can't be forty (fo**u**rty)
or
Forty soldiers stormed the fort.

---

because

see the -au- in bec**au**se

bec a use

always understand

Or remember a word in the word in beca**use** - **use**
Use *this because you'll **a**lways **u**nderstand.*

necessary/unnecessary
Use sayings to help with the difficult 'c' and 's' letters.

It's necessary to have 1 Collar and 2 Sleeves.

1 Collar

2 Sleeves

neCeSSary

or *It's neCeSSary to Cut Some Services.*

accessory (two c's and 2 s's)
A Charming Chain in Shiny Silver <u>or y</u>ellow gold is a good access<u>ory</u>.
Acce**pt the **accessory.
*accessor**ies** (change the **y** to **ies**)*

Also *accessorise* (BrE) or *accessorize* (AmE and BrE).

occasion (2 c's and 1 s)
*On special o**cc**a**s**ions I have **C**offee, **C**ream and **S**ugar.*

Also *occasional occasionally*
occasion + al = *occasional* + ly = *occasionally*

accident   *When two **c**ars **c**ollide they make a **dent**.*
Or, ***A C**ar **C**rashed made a **dent**.*

fluorescent (begins with fluor-) *flu or e scent*
*I had the **flu** and **s**pent the night in a fluorescent **tent**.*
-escent pattern: *adol**escent**, lumin**escent**, obsol**escent**, phosphorescent, incandescent, convalescent.*

embarrass/embarrassed/embarrassing/embarrassment
Tricky: double 'r' and double 's'

She has Really Red cheeks because she's Seriously Shy and embaRRaSSed.

Do you go Really Red and Smile Shyly when you're embarrassed?

harass/harassment (*Don't get *harass* confused with *embarrass**)
Just one 'r' and double 's'
*Ha, how **crass** to ha**rass**.*
*You don't have the **right** to ha**rass**, you **ass**!*

"ass" words
assistant *The assistant is an ass.*
An ass and an ant are my assistants.
assassin *An assassin is a double ass.*
harass *He's an ass and crass to harass.*
embarrass *I go really red and so shy when I'm embarrassed and feel like an ass.*

Think of some suitable "ass" sentences for these words:

assault	associate/association
assignment	assume
assembly/assemble	

---

friend *Put your* **friend** *before the* **end**. fr i end
I always visit my **friend** *on* **Fridays**.
Let's have **fries** *with friends on* **Friday**.

Caribbean = Carib bean "Ca rib be an"
There are **really** **beautiful** **beaches** *in the* **Caribbean**.

receive *It's better to* **give** *than* **receive**.

perseverance
*If you have per**severa**nce you are willing to do something*
several *times before you get it right.*

knowledge *Knowledge gives you the* **edge**.

truly is a common misspelled word
true (drop the 'e') + ly = truly   *It's* **truly** *hot in* **July**.

minuscule This word comes from **minute** (tiny), so minuscule.

millennium (double 'l' and double 'n') Double 'l' like *million*.
Breaks down into syllables well – "mill/en/ni/um"

laugh *Laugh and you get happy.*

occurred *The car crash occurred in a hurry.*
occurrence *I dread the occurrence of a* **Car Crashing** *and*
Running **Right** *into my* **fence** (a bit long, but I need to
remember the –ence ending somehow). Can you think of a
better sentence?

Also see the pattern in *occur*   *recur*   *blur*
double up the 'r'   *occurring* *recurring* *blurring*
                       occurred   *recurred*   *blurred*

(More info about this doubling up rule in the Spelling Rules
section)

accommodation/accommodate(s)/accommodating (drop 'e' with -ing)

The problem with this word is usually with the **c's** and **m's**.

Use syllable breakdown: ac/com/mo/da/tion
Or, better still, use a memory trick and sentence linked to *accommodation.*

The accommodation has 2 cots and 2 mattresses.
The accommodation has 2 cradles and 2 mattresses.

2 <u>C</u>ots   2 <u>C</u>ots
 2 <u>M</u>attresses   2 <u>M</u>attresses

accOmmOdation

Don't forget the 2 o's – 2 rOund babies.
Now we have twins, our accommodation needs two cots and two mattresses for our 2 round babies.

Or
The accommodation has 2 cats and 2 mice.

More tricky **mm**'s

dilemma *Emma is in a dilemma.*
flammable *Grass gets flammable in summer.*
immediately = immediate + ly
I ate my meal immediately.
I ate the m & m's ® immediately.

We'll also see some double m's when adding the prefix –im to
a root word beginning with 'm'.
im + mature = *immature*   im + migrant = *immigrant*
immaterial, immeasurable, immodest, immobile...

We'll also see double 'm' in the 1:1:1 doubling up rule in the
spelling rules section:
swim – *swimmer, swimming, swimmable*
slim – *slimmer, slimming, slimmest*

-comm- + vowel
committee - *Many meetings take time – everyone's
exhausted.*
commit**tee** - *coffee, settee*
communicate/**communication** – *Mass media is now our
communication.*
community - *A summer community.*
commission - *Come to the mission.*
comma - *Comma errors are common.*
recommend re + commend = recommend
recommendation/recommending

Write a letter pattern story or sentences.

55

com + p words

Notice these "comp" words have one **m**.

They easily breakdown into syllables "com pet i tion"

compete/competition

complete/completely "com plete" Notice the e's.

complete + ly = *completely*

complain "com plain"

comparison *Paris is beyond comparison.*

compatible

competent

complacent

complexion *I have a complex complexion.*

The "h**app**y" words

apparently *You're apparently happy about the rent.*

appearance *Your appearance at the dance made him happy.*

appetite *I'm happy my pet's appetite is back.*

appointment *This is a happy appointment.*

appreciate *I appreciate being happy.*

appropriate *The apple I ate was appropriate.*

approve / approval *Their approval makes me happy.*

dis + app

disapprove, disapproval

disappoint, disappointed, disappointment,

disappear, disappeared, disappearance

Write some sentences and stories

56

Nouns ending in -acy and -asy

ecstasy "ek" sta sy   ec sta sy

It has the same beginning sound as <u>ex</u>tra, so don't be confused and put 'x'. And don't forget the 's' before 'c' ecs tasy.

Only four words end in **-asy**:
ecstasy, fantasy, idiosyncrasy, apostasy

Change the -tic to -y
fantastic – fantasy

Change the -tic to -sy
ecstatic – ecstasy, idiosyncratic - idiosyncrasy

The **-acy** ending is much more common: *privacy, immediacy, legacy, fallacy, lunacy, intimacy, delicacy, pharmacy*

These endings are "**racy**": *demo**cracy**, literacy, bureaucracy, piracy, accuracy, conspiracy, numeracy, aristocracy*

Change the -t/-te to -cy
*deli**cate** – delicacy, nume**rate** – numeracy, literate – literacy, **pirate** – piracy, immediate – immediacy, intimate – intimacy, accurate – accuracy, democrat – democracy, bureaucrat – bureaucracy, aristocrat - aristocracy*

-sede, -ceed, -cede

supersede is the only word ending in **-sede**.
This word literally means to sit on top of something (to replace it). So **super** is "on top of" and **sede** is "sit", so think of *sit* for the 's' in **sede** (not cede) or **sede**ntary.

Words ending in the same sound are **-ceed** and **-cede**.
Only 3 words end in **-ceed**: *exceed, succeed, proceed*

-cede: *concede, precede, recede, intercede, accede, secede*

First letters

Make up a saying using the first letters of the word. If it's related to the meaning, all the better.

chaos *cyclones, hurricanes and other storms create chaos*

rhythm Say to yourself when spelling it *"rhythm has your two hips moving."* (I use this all the time; it takes some effort to remember these, but it's worth it.)

rhyme *rhyme helps your memory expand*

because
big elephants can always understand small elephants
Or, *be ever careful and use sharp eyes*

diarrhoea (BrE)
dash in a real rush, hurry or else accident
Or, *dining in a rough restaurant: hurry or expect accidents!*

diarrhea (AmE)
dash in a real rush, hurry else accident
Or, *Dining in a rough restaurant: hurry expect accidents!*

laugh *laugh and u get happy*

Wednesday *We do not eat soup day*

biscuits *I love biscuits crumbled up into tiny piece*

liaison – *live in an igloo, son*

Exercise

Which is correct? Use your visual memory, memory tricks and words within words to help you. If you're not sure, that's fine, look back over the words and tricks.

1. a. harrass   b. harass

2. a. tommorrow   b. tomorrow

3. a. dillema   b. dilemma

4. a. supercede   b. supersede

5. a. minuscule   b. miniscule

6. a. asignment   b. assignment

7. a. appointment   b. apointment

8. a. apparently   b. apparantly

9. a. completely   b. commpletely

10. a. comittee   b. committee

11. a. ecstacy   b. ecstasy

12. a. occurred   b. ocurred

13. a. unneccessary   b. unnecessary

14. a. forty   b. fourty

15. a. acknowledge   b. acknowlege

16. a. rythmn   b. rhythm

Exercise Answers

1. a. harrass   b. harass

2. a. tommorrow   b. tomorrow

3 a. dillema   b. dilemma

4. a. supercede   b. supersede

5. a. minuscule   b. miniscule

6. a. asignment   b. assignment

7. a. appointment   b. apointment

8. a. apparently   b. apparantly

9. a. completely   b. commpletely

10. a. comittee   b. committee

11. a. ecstacy   b. ecstasy

12. a. occurred   b. ocurred

13 a. unneccessary   b. unnecessary

14. a. forty   b. fourty

15. a. acknowledge   b. acknowlege

16 a. rythmn   b. rhythm

Spotting Vowels

In this lesson, we'll look at the importance of seeing vowels in words, especially in words like *separate, definitely, relevant, cemetery*. We'll also revise some of the other words and strategies used so far in the previous lessons.

This is a great strategy for people with dyslexia. According to beatingdyslexia.com: "Vowels are harder to clearly define than consonants. The vowels can cause greater confusion due to the variety of ways the letters can represent the sounds. This is why focusing on only the vowels can make spelling easier."

Quote from www.beatingdyslexia.com
www.beatingdyslexia.com/vowel-lessons.html

Focus on only the vowels: *When I'm learning to spell a new word the first thing I do is focus on only the vowels. I remember misspelling the word sentence. If we look at only the vowels in the word 'sentence', we can see they are all **e**'s.*

s**e**nt**e**nc**e**

Sometimes, the meaning of a word can give us a clue to the vowel letter patterns.
*A **beach** is by the **sea**.*
*A **beech** is a **tree**.*
*A cal**en**dar is a list of **dates**.*
***Hear** with your **ear** and **learn**.*

Can you see the vowels in these words?
cemetery
people
independent
irresistible

cemetery ce me te ry
See all the e's:
*A cemetery is **eerie** with lots of greenery not evil.*

discipline (notice all those i's) dis cip line

people pe O ple   pe ⌣ ple

existence ex is tence

independent in de pen dent   independence
*The independ**ent** voters didn't make **enough** of a **dent**.*

irresistible ir res is ti ble
Your new lip<u>st</u>ick makes you irresistible.

separate sep a rate   or *Separate a rat.*

tendency ten den cy

remember re mem ber

Also e's in September Sep tem ber
                    December De cem ber

liaise, liaison li a ise, li a is on

visible *2 i's (eyes) are visible*

significant sig nif i cant   sign if I can't

qualification qua li fi ca tion

museum mu se um
Notice the 'u' either side of the 'e'?

various i.o.u various gifts   I o (owe) u (you)

queue Four vowels in a queue! **queue**

weird Well **weird!**

'ie' or 'ei' patterns

One very common rule to remember some of the **'ie'** and **'ei'** words like *receive, achieve, receipt, ceiling* is using the rhyme: "'i' before 'e' except after a long 'c'".

'ie' patterns "ee" sound
'i' before 'e' = *achieve, mischief, mischievous, believe, relief, unbelievable, achievable, piece, niece, field, chief, thief...*
Exception = *weird*

'ei' patterns "ee" sound
'i' before 'e' except after a long 'c' = *receive, receipt, ceiling, conceive, deceit...*

'ie' patterns "shu" sounds
'i' before 'e' when 'c' is a "sh" sound = *ancient, patient, proficient, efficient*

'ei' patterns
'e' before 'i' when sounded like "ay" = *neighbour/neighbor, weigh, eight, freight, beige, veil...*

There are 7 sounds for 'ie' and 'ei' patterns:

1. the "ee" sound as in "green" (*relief, field, receive, weird*)
2. the "ay" sound as in "pay" (*weigh, eight, vein*)
3. the "i" sound as in "hit" (*foreign, counterfeit*)
4. the "eye" sound as in "ice" (*height, feisty*)
5. the "eh" sound as in "best" (*leisure, friend*)
6. the "uh" sound as in "hunt" (*patient, ancient*)
7. the "oo" sound as in "shoe" (*view, review, in lieu*)

You might not remember the rules but see the patterns instead.

Exercise. Fill in the missing 'ei' or '-ie'

anc__nt, pat__nt, profic__nt, effic__nt

w__gh, __ght, v__l

h__ght

rel__f, rec__ve, rec__ving

ach__ve, ach__vable

conc__ve, concei__t, rec__pt

bel__ve, bel__f, bel__ving

Exercise. Fill in the missing vowels

pe__ple

bel__ __ve

rec__ __ve

l__a__son

acc__mm__dation

s__nt__nc__

S__pt__mb__r

r__m__mb__r

D__c__mb__r

s__tisf__ct__ry

m__se__m

w__ird

c__lend__r

Exercise Answers Fill in the missing 'ei' or '-ie'

ancient, patient, proficient, efficient

weigh, eight, veil

height

relief, receive, receiving

achieve, achievable

conceive, conceit, receipt

believe, belief, believing

Exercise Answers

people

believe

receive

liaison

accommodation

sentence

September

remember

December

satisfactory

museum

weird

calendar

Silent Letters

know, two, Wednesday, eight, knee, write, listen, could, walk... All these common words have silent letters in them. Can you remember why we have silent letters?

More than 60% of English words have silent letters in them, which can cause all sorts of problems spelling the word, pronouncing the word, or looking for the word in a dictionary.

Memory tricks

Wednesday
We say "wensday", so if you're relying on pronunciation, it won't help. But we can use syllable breakdown to help. Break the word down slowly and exaggeratedly when writing it - "Wed" "nes" "day". This helps you remember the silent 'd' and 'e' (more details in the Syllable section).

island *An island is **land** surrounded by water.*

write *Write Words.*

Words within words

business *Going by **bus** is good for **business**.*

listen *Please **listen** to the **list**.*

See links between words

know - *knowing* – *knows* - *knowledge* - *knowledgeable* – *acknowledge* – *acknowledgement*

*Kn**OW**ledge is p**OW**er.*

two – *twelve* – *twenty* - *twins* – *twice* – *twelfth*

sign – *signal* – *signpost* - *signing* – *signature* - *signify*
resign – *resigning* – *resignation*   *design* – *designer*

See the patterns and write sentences with the pattern.

guitar, guilty, guide, guidance, fruit juice
I only play the guitar when drinking fruit juice in a suit.

light, right, bright, flight, sight, might, fright
I had a fright last night when my light went out.

More on these letter patterns, letter pattern stories, word families and word links in later sections.

Little dinosaurs!

Remember that silent letters are fossilized dinosaurs of a once spoken letter. So let's look at the history of them and some rules.

One of the most useful strategies to improve spelling is knowing why spelling is the way it is (etymological system). So knowing why we have so many words with silent letters in them will not only help your spelling, reading, and pronunciation, but stop you getting frustrated with spelling.

English and spelling developed from the languages of the invaders that settled in England. Each time the country was invaded, so too was English and spelling.

43 AD - the **Romans** from Italy (spoke Latin)

410 AD - the **Angles, Saxons, Jutes** from Germany and Holland (spoke Dutch/Germanic)

793 AD - the **Vikings** from Denmark and Norway (spoke Old Norse)

1066 AD - the **French** (spoke Norman French)

In 43 AD, the Romans invaded and colonized Britain. They spoke Latin. We still use some Roman Latin words - look at these with silent letters in them: *scissors, salmon, debt, receipt, plumber.*

410 AD, the Anglo-Saxons

The Romans withdrew from Britain, and the **Anglo-Saxons** invaded from Germany and Holland. These Saxons, Angles and Jutes spoke a number of Germanic languages (west Germanic and Dutch) that eventually became Anglo-Saxon - **English!**

The 100 most common words in present day English are from Anglo-Saxon, including everyday words: *earth, house, food, sing, night, daughter, night, women, light, cough, sleep...*

The history of -gh-:

- The 'h' in the original spelling was a hard throaty sound, like the Scottish sound in *loch.*
- Then around the 13th century 'g' was added to 'h', becoming 'gh', because of the French influence to try to spell this throaty sound.
- Then in about the 17th century, the 'gh' sound became silent: *night, daughter, though, through, plough, borough, slaughter.*
  Or, became the "f" sound: *enough, cough, tough, rough, laugh...*

We have gh- at the beginning of words, but this pattern was introduced much later by Dutch/Flemish influenced printers: *ghost, ghastly, ghetto, gherkin, Ghent...*

-gh- letter pattern word search.
Words can also be upside down, vertical, horizontal, backwards

```
r a e r t r h u h j b z j t y q e a h r
a v i k j h g i d g o r h p w t h g i r
w m g z e q u m a e u o i e n t o a w r
y s h j r p o x o z u o i g h c l g j x
k l t u y p r c l g j g r i h f x f m u
q c d k g a h d h e h u g d c t y b w i
d z s g e u t z v t r h t u j j d o l x
f n j d s l l p n w y b l i a r m a z a
b n u r x z z v q i k i e z s a o w x w
b s s n b g y a l q j c d y n t f h u b
e e j x w q u m z b l l z c v y g i a r
z v w d s q q l f c r p i h j i o t k p
n i g h t m q b v i o f u g h m k d g t
w h h j f u g m b s i w i a h g p s n h
j d b g w t f e i h w v y m g t f e s x
j o k s l c t q o n g c a s t w u i j b
j h l c w o k n u a n u t l g j z z f b
l i h l u i h p k c h a o h l s q v y k
l e v g e d i y z g r e y c q r s y c d
z g h e m r k i g w p l z t a h i e n p
```

bright	cough	eight	though
high	light	~~night~~	through
right	rough	thigh	tough
weight			

793 AD, the Vikings

The Vikings from Denmark and Norway invaded. They gave English loads of words, including the silent letter words: *knife, knock, knee, know, gnat, gnaw,* gnash... The silent 'k' and 'g' used to be pronounced, but in the 17th century began to drop out of fashion.

The Anglo-Saxon and Viking languages became Old English.

1066 AD, the Norman French

The Norman French invaded and French was spoken in law, and by the ruling classes for 300 years! Anglo-Saxon (English) was spoken by peasants and the suppressed - it survived! The French gave us an enormous vocabulary of words, but they changed a lot of our spellings to fit in with theirs. Let's look at a couple of silent letters.

-gu-

The French put a silent **U** in words like **guess** because in French **g** followed by **e** would sound like "j". So 'gu' made it a "k" sound: *guide, guess, guilty, guard, guarantee, dialogue...*

gest (Old English) to **gu**est
tunge (Old English) to tongue
vage (Old English) to vague
voge (Old English) to vogue

But –gu- in these words are a "gw" sound
anguish, distinguish, extinguish, languish, linguistic, penguin

The Letter H

The pronunciation of the letter H on some words can be silent or pronounced, depending on your accent.

For centuries, this letter wasn't pronounced, especially when the words came from French: *habit, history, honest, hospital, hotel...*

By the 18th century, H began to be pronounced in some words but not others. H was silent in *habit, harmonious, heritage, heir, herb, honest, humour/humor* and certain other words. Some of these words are now pronounced with the H in some accents.

Words that still have a silent H are of French origin: *heir, honest, honour/honor, hour, herb* (in American). This is useful to know, because when you write 'a' or 'an', you add 'an' for a silent 'h'. *In an hour's time.*
A historical event but *an honest approach.*

Academics and silent letters

The academics of the Renaissance in the 16th century were very enthusiastic about Classical Latin and Greek, which they thought of as intellectual. They borrowed words from these languages to express new concepts: *chaos, democracy, encyclopedia, pneumonia.*

They also wanted to imitate some Latin spellings to give English spellings more "authority", so they shoved in those troublesome silent letters!

- **Doubt** (silent b) is a mix of Old French *doute* and Latin *dubitare.*
- **Debt** (silent b) is from the Latin *debitum.*
- **Subtle** (silent b) is from the Latin *subtilem.*
- **Receipt** (silent p) is a combination of Anglo/Norman French *receite* and Latin *recepta.*
- **Scissors** (silent c) was *sisoures,* but then a c was added because of the Latin *scindere* to split.
- **Salmon** (silent l) was *samon,* then they added the silent 'l' to show its classical roots.

These words were originally logically spelt before the academics messed about with them and increased their complexity!

They sometimes increased the number of irregular forms: the Old English **gh** of *night* and *light* was added to *delight* and *tight.*

I go into more detail about the history of spelling in my book, *The Reasons Why English is so Weird and Wonderful.*

Another three reasons why silent letters are in words:

1. Silent letters help the reader to recognize the difference between homophones: *in/inn, knot/not, to/too/two, know/no, whole/hole, lent/leant, write/right...*

2. A silent letter can help us work out the meaning of the word and can change the pronunciation, even though it's silent: *sin/sign,* and the important silent 'e' to make a long vowel sound in *rat/rate, mad/made, tap/tape.*

3. Most silent letters which used to be pronounced became silent over the centuries, but the letters were left in the spellings because printing had "fixed" them.

Pronunciation always changes. Even now, we shorten words, slide letters together, chop letters off - all to make speaking easier, and a nightmare for spelling!

Next up, we have some silent letter rules.

Can you see the rules in these words?

write, wrong, wreck
knife, knock, knee
crumb, lamb, comb
palm, calm, salmon
walk, talk, yolk
damn, autumn, column

Silent letter patterns and rules

kn- silent **k** before **n**: _kn_ee, know, knife, knives, knob, knobbly, knot, knuckle, knock, knack, knave, knead, kneel, knew, knit...

gn- silent **g** before **n**: _gn_at, gnaw, gnash, gnarl, gnome...

-gn- a*lign*, assign, benign, design, malign, reign, sign, campaign, poignant, champagne, cologne, foreign...

wr- silent **w** before **r**: _wr_ite, wrist, wrinkle, wring, wriggle, wrong, wrote, wrap, wreck, wrench, wrestle (silent w, t, e!)

ps- silent **p** before **s**: _ps_ychic, psalm, psychology, psychiatry...

-lk silent **l** before **k**: fo_lk_, walk, talk, yolk, chalk...

-mb- silent **b** after **m**: plu_mb_er, numb, dumb, thumb, crumb, climb, limb, lamb, succumb, bomb, comb, tomb, womb...

-mn silent **n** after **m**: autu_mn_, column, solemn, condemn, damn, hymn...

-lm- silent **l** before **m**: palm, calm, psalm (silent p & l), qualm, alms, almond, balm, salmon...

-st- silent **t** after **s**: li_st_en, fasten, glisten, moisten, hasten...

-stle bristle, bustle, castle, gristle, hustle, jostle, mistletoe, rustle, thistle, whistle, wrestle (silent w/t)

The silent **l** in three important words: would, could, should

You could make up a sentence with words starting with silent letters:
I guessed the guitar was under guarantee.
The knight knew the knack of knitting knickers.

You may already know how to spell one or two of the words. Putting them together means you are linking something new to something you already know.

Anne Betteridge: *Adult Learners' Guide to Spelling.*

Write some silent letter pattern stories.
The gnarled gnome gnashed his teeth as he gnawed a gnat.
The plumber climbed the old tomb but it crumbled, and he broke his thumb which now felt numb.
I tried to knead the knot out of the knitting but didn't know how so I cut it with a knife but cut my knuckle instead.

Notes
Now you write some silent letter pattern stories or sentences

Silent to sounded

Consonants that are silent in some words are sometimes pronounced/sounded in a related word; for example, *sign.* but *signal, signature.* This is probably to aid pronunciation.

To remember the spelling of a word with a silent letter, try to think of a word related in spelling and meaning, and you might get a clue from the consonant that is pronounced.

silent - pronounced
bomb - bombard, bombardment
condemn - condemnation
Christmas - Christ
crumb - crumble, crumbling
damn - damnation
design - designate
fasten - fast
hasten - haste
malign - malignant
moisten - moist
muscle - muscular
limb - limber
resign - resignation
sign - signal, signature
soften - soft, softly
solemn – solemnity
knowledge - acknowledge

Careful: *numb* and its comparative adjective *number* are silent - *My numb thumb is number than before.* But we have the voiced "b" in *number* one, *numbers.*

Exercise. Silent letters in body parts

1. Write in the missing letter

a: ___nee   b: ___rist   c: pa ___m   d: shou ___der

e: thum_____   f: mus___les

2. Write in the missing words

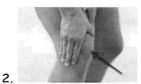

1. This is a _____

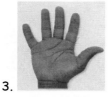

2. This is a _____

3. This is the _____ of the hand.

4. This is a _____

5. He's building up his _____

Exercise Answers

1. Write in the missing letter

a: **k**nee   b: **w**rist   c: pa**l**m   d: shou**l**der   e: thum**b**

f: mus**c**les

2. Write in the missing words

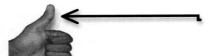

1.   This is a <u>thumb.</u>

2.   This is a <u>knee.</u>

3.   This is the <u>palm</u> of the hand.

4.   This is a <u>wrist.</u>

5.   He's building up his <u>muscles.</u>

Sound-Alikes - Homophones

there/they're/their, to/too/two, right/write,
been/bean
witch/which, bye/buy/by, here/hear, it's/its,
pear/pair/pare
new/knew, piece/peace, genes/jeans, here/hear...

homophones = words that have the same sound but different meaning and different spelling.

homophone comes from the Greek words:
homos = same and *phone* = sound

I want to buy that pear **or** *I want to buy that pair*
Thinking allowed **or** *Thinking aloud*
I rode around the lake **or** *I rowed around the lake*

If you write, "We need too right a letter," the spell-checker will not detect a misspelling. In terms of writing done on a computer, such homophone errors are the most common type of misspelling, sometimes the only type you might see in a word-processed document.

One way to avoid these misspellings is to be aware of the most common homophones and proofread carefully when using them. Work on the ones that confuse you the most, and if in two weeks you can thoroughly remember the difference between three or four homophone errors, that would be an important victory.

Professor Larry Beason: *Eyes before Ease*

Using memory tricks to help you figure out which homophone is which is so important. I use strategies like seeing words within words, and sayings to help me, especially when going over my work to check if I've used the correct one.

> People from every walk of life, regardless of their educational level and background, make mistakes when spelling words such as "principle" and "principal", "desert" and "dessert", "stationery" and "stationary", as well as dozens of other every day, same-sounding words, i.e. homophones. http://www.4sliteracy.com.au/publications14.asp

Homophones are tricky because the computer won't tell you if you've used the wrong one. So proofreading even the shortest of emails, and going over every piece of writing, is so important. I've been caught out with predictive text too and just pressed send, and when I looked back over a Facebook comment, cringed. I mean really cringed at a spelling error, or wrong word, not too good for a spelling expert!

- Don't just press send.
- Go over your work carefully.
- Read it aloud and slowly to see if you've missed any small words and endings.
- Are the notoriously tricky homophone words right? (Use spelling strategies to check whether they're right.)

You should go over every single word and sentence you type, not only because of stupid predictive text but, when you type fast, the first homophone that pops in your head will usually be the one you type, especially when you want to get your feelings and thoughts out without thinking about spelling. That's why proofreading these words is so important. Even the most accomplished speller and writer, myself included, goes over their work before pressing send.

Homophones are one of the biggest mistakes I used to make in my writing, so I'm very mindful of them, and use tricks to help me see if I've used the correct one.

Using visual clues, memory tricks, dictionary definitions, and sentences will help you learn these words and hopefully write them automatically.

The context of the word can help you decide which homophone should be used. For example, *a home can be for sale*, while *a boat can have a sail*. Or, we need more information: *I want to buy that pear* or *I want to buy that pair*. A juicy pear to eat, or a pair of shoes?

Look at this sentence: *Please send me a peace of you're work.*

All the words are spelled correctly so the spellchecker on your computer won't tell you they're misspelled. Can you spot the mistakes?

The sentence should be: *Please send me a **piece** of **your** work.*

Exercise

Proofread these sentences. Are they correct or wrong?

1. Do you no were there from?

2. I'd like a peace of cake.

3. I'm hear on business.

4. You're car is blocking mine.

5. What's going on over their?

6. My son needs sum stationary for college.

Exercise Answers

Proofread these sentences and correct the mistakes

1. Do you ~~no were there~~ <u>know where they're</u> from?

2. I'd like a ~~peace~~ <u>piece</u> of cake.

3. I'm ~~hear~~ <u>here</u> on business.

4. ~~You're~~ <u>Your</u> car is blocking mine.

5. What's going on over ~~their~~ <u>there</u>?

6. My son needs ~~sum~~ <u>some</u> ~~stationary~~ <u>stationery</u> for college.

Using memory tricks to help you remember which word is which is one of the best strategies to help you. When you use a memory trick, especially words within words, it's best if you link the difficult bit with something connected with the word's meaning.

Let's look at some very common homophone mistakes, and possible memory tricks to use.

peace/piece

Can you remember the word within the word in *piece*?

This is a *pi**ece** of **pie***.
There's a pie in piece.

P**eace** is **ace**.
Peace of mind is ace.
*pe**ace** **and** love.*

aloud/allowed

*Y**ou** are so l**oud** so stop talking al**oud***
Will we be allowed in?

*If y**ou** keep on talking **aloud**, you wi**ll** not be **allowed** to stay.*

whether/weather

*You can only **eat** out in good **weather**.*
*Whether you get **het** up or not is up to you!*
Why? When? What? Whether or not?
***Whether** or not the **weather** is good or **whether** it's bad,*
we'll go.

> **Poem**
> *Whether the weather is fine,*
> *Whether the weather is not,*
> *We must weather the weather,*
> *Whatever the weather,*
> *Whether we like it or not.*
> Anon

hear/here

here = place
Can you see the **here** in these words about place?
T**here**, w**here**, everyw**here**, now**here**.
*Where is it? It's **here**!*

Can you see the word within **hear** that relates to hearing?
*Hear with your **ear** and **learn**.*
hear, hears, hearing, heard

See the **ear** letter pattern in this sentence (remember
letter patterns can have different sounds):
*The **bear** likes to **wear** **ear**rings on each **ear**.*

write/right

Write **W**ords

*I need to **Write** **Words** right when **Writing**.*

writing – drop the 'e' with –ing writ~~e~~ ➜ writing
right = correct ✓ or turn right
*I write with my rig**ht** **h**and.*

82

new/knew

knew links with *know, knew, knowledge*
new rhymes with *new, few, blew, screw*

*I **knew** she was going to wear her **new** coat.*

through/threw
*He **threw** it **through** the window.*
*I walked **through** the park and then **through** town.*
*I **threw** the new ball (**threw** is the past tense of **throw**).*

your/you're
your = possession: *my, his, her, your, their,* **our** house, **your** house. See the **our** in **your**.
This is **ours**. That is **yours**.

you're is the short form/contraction of ***you are***. The apostrophe replaces the 'a' and joins the two words together.

you're = you are

Do you like your work?/Do you like you're work?
Do you like your work? Say out loud "my" or "our" for **your** -
Do you like "my" "our" your work? ✓
*Do you like **you're** work? Do you like **you are** work?* X (wrong)

Which is correct?
a. I hope you and your family are well.
b. I hope your and your family are well.
c. I hope you and you're family are well.

---

there/their/they're

there = place = ***here, there, where, there is, there are, there was, there were, is there/are there?***
their = possession = *my car, their car.* *Their – I = my - their*
they're is a contraction of *they are,* so when reading your work back, say *they're* as *they are* and you'll soon see if it's correct.

Which one is correct?

a. *There is a problem over at they're place.*
b. *They're is a problem over at there place.*
c. *There is a problem over at their place.*

where/were/we're

where = place and relates to *here, there, where*
Also *where is/are/was/were*

were is the past tense of *are*
you were, they were, we were
(I was, he was, she was)

we're = we are **We're** *(We are) going to the park*

Where were you yesterday? The children **were** looking forward to seeing you.

Which is correct?

a. *Where were you yesterday?*
b. *Where we're you yesterday?*
c. *Were where you yesterday?*

waist/waste

I have a 22-inch waist.
The waiter has a narrow waist.
I hate waste.
Don't waste the paste in haste.

guest/guessed

guest *She's a tourist and guest.*

guessed is the past tense of to **guess**
I guessed it right. She guessed/He guessed/They/We/You guessed

What's the problem with this sign?

stationery or **stationary?**
The photo should have station<u>e</u>ry with an <u>e</u>.

Station<u>e</u>ry = <u>e</u>nvelopes pens, paper...
Station<u>a</u>ry = at the station, a station<u>a</u>ry c<u>a</u>r

Station<u>e</u>ry = <u>e</u>nvelopes

Station<u>a</u>ry c<u>a</u>rs

principle/principal
The *principle* rule.
The school principal is not your pal.

desert/dessert
Desert is sand.
Dessert is sweet stuff

If you have a problem with which homophone to use then use a memory trick to help you.

Notes

Answers to the exercises

a. I hope you and your family are well.
b. I hope your and your family are well. x
c. I hope you and you're family are well. x

a. There is a problem over at they're place x
b. They're is a problem over at there place x
c. There is a problem over at their place.

a. Where were you yesterday? (past tense)
b. Where we're you yesterday? x
c. Were where you yesterday? x

Exercise

1. We had lunch over at (there/their/they're) house.

2. (Where/Were/We're) are you from?

3. I always walk (through/threw) the park to get to work.

4. I (no/know) what you want and the answer is (no/know).

5. (Their/There/They're) grandmother used to live over (their/there/they're).

6. Use to/too/two
   It is _____ early _____ collect my children from

   school so I'm going _____ the shops _____ buy

   _____ cakes for them.

7. (There/Their/They're) not thinking about (there/their/they're) future because (there/their/they're) (to/too/two) young (to/too/two) care.

8. (Where/We're/Were) going to the beach today.

9. I hope (you're/your) phone's OK and (its/it's) battery isn't damaged.

Exercise Answers

1. We had lunch over at (their) house.

2. (Where) are you from?

3. I always walk (through) the park to get to work.

4. I (know) what you want and the answer is (no).

5. (Their) grandmother used to live over (there).

6. Use to/too/two
   It is <u>too</u> early <u>to</u> collect my children from school so I'm going <u>to</u> the shops to buy <u>two</u> cakes for them.

7. (They're) not thinking about (their) future because (they're) (too) young (to) care.

8. (We're) going to the beach today.

9. I hope (your) phone's OK and (its) battery isn't damaged.

Some interesting sound-alike endings

-ical and -icle patterns

-ical = adjectives (describing words)
comical, magical, logical, illogical, musical, astronomical, farcical, biblical, technical, typical, medical, critical, radical, vertical, physical, mechanical, mathematical, whimsical...

These words usually have a root word ending in **-ic**, so just add **-al**: comic + al = *comical*, magic + al = *magical*, medic/al, physic/al, mathematic/al...

We can add **-ly** to these words *magically, comically, logically...*

-icle words = nouns
icicle, vehicle, article, particle, cubicle, cuticle, testicle, follicle...

-er, -ar, -or endings

-er patterns
singer, teacher, actor, doctor, regular, pillar, author

For most accents, the *-er -or -ar* endings are an unstressed "a" sound or "schwa", which is the most common sound in English.

-er has the most endings
Verbs ending in silent 'e' add 'r': *dive/diver, write/writer, drive/driver, love/lover...*

-er is the most common ending for someone carrying out an action or job: *swim/swimmer, report/reporter, play/player, fight/fighter, email/emailer, do/doer, drink/drinker...*

We use **-er** for comparative adjectives
bigger, braver, smaller, better, larger...

We use **-er** for these months: *September, October, November, December*

-or patterns and rules

-or endings are used when the root word ends in -ct, -it, -ate, -ess, -rr:

act – *actor*
collect – *collector*
reflect – *reflector*
detect – *detector*
conduct – *conductor*

inspect – *inspector*
contract – *contractor*
instruct – *instructor*
constrict – *constrictor*
tractor, convector, prospector

-ator is the largest group of -or words

Drop the 'e' and add 'or'

create – *creator*
operate – *operator*
moderate – *moderator*
investigate – *investigator*
regulate – *regulator*
spectate – *spectator*
navigate – *navigator*

calculate – *calculator*
radiate – *radiator*
educate – *educator*
translate – *translator*
illustrate – *illustrator*
doctorate – doctor
curate – *curator*

-itor

visit – *visitor*
exhibit – *exhibitor*

edit – *editor*
inhibit – *inhibitor*

deposit – *depositor*
credit – *creditor*

-essor

professor, process – processor, compress – compressor
predecessor

Also: *sponsor, supervisor, advisor*
advise – advisor

-rror

error, terror, horror, mirror

-ror

conjuror, conqueror, emperor

-lar patterns

We usually use 'ar' after 'l'

-ular adjectives (pronunciation may help)

regular, popular, circular, modular, triangular ,vehicular, particular,
molecular, jocular...
similar, solar, scholar,
collar, dollar, cellar, caterpillar,
familiar, peculiar (liar liar, he's a *familiar peculiar* liar)

But also: *sugar, beggar, calendar, vinegar, jaguar, vulgar, tsar/czar*
sonar, lunar

Exercise
Using your knowledge of –er, –or, –ar endings fill in the letter.

1. adapt___r

2. commut___r

3. elevat___r

4. regul___r

5. horr___r

6. subscrib___r

7. tut___r

8. commentat___r

9. famili_r

10. popul_r

Exercise answers

1. adaptor 2. commuter 3. elevator 4. regular
5. horror 6. subscriber 7. tutor 8. commentator
9. familiar 10. popular

Word search – find the jobs. Words can also be upside down, vertical, horizontal, backwards.

```
w x i h p a d m m r k e z d f t r i p n
p c c p x g r b c s o y o w t e n c r c
m b u a f o e g r u o s s m v s q y d y
t g h q v k t j y e s x s i p x o i q f
i r z z e q r z p k g d d e c x y z g l
k v a o k b o f p a h n c q f d b l a o
f o g n o k p q d t r t i o d o m f d b
z l i w s c e r g e o r j s c k r b v v
g s p w q l r f h r c u r a t o r p i v
x s c i u b a c r o t c o d o n z o s b
j u s h x s a t u t d k t w c r p l o r
d p o b o e y z o z c e v l e c u p r a
w e q m t l r o g r z m l u x f w w w g
w r d v d b a t p e e c y h m h h r w g
i v j f p t m r g m f b y n z k i b a e
k i r a c m u w h x v d o b q t e n n b
p s i n v e s t i g a t o r e o u p t a
v o j c j u p e u t k y g r f q t m r y
v r u v v p j l b v y b j n j r f f s n
r o t c u d n o c c r p m s p o k v x y
```

advisor   ~~reporter~~
beggar   conductor
curator   diver
doctor   inspector
investigator   professor
scholar   singer
supervisor   teacher
translator   writer

92

-ette and -et

-ette The ending was borrowed from French along with a lot of the "ette" words. You can also add it to other words to make new words.

kitchenette, luncheonette, maisonette, brunette, marionette, baguette, silhouette, etiquette, pirouette, statuette, leatherette, launderette, vinaigrette, novelette, towelette, flannelette, Gillette, palette, roulette, cassette, rosette, corvette, serviette

Female names: *Annette, Antoinette, Bernadette, Bette, Collette, Janette, Yvette, Odette*

Some of the words indicate the feminine gender:
suffragette, drum majorette, usherette

British vs. American differences
serviette (napkin)
courgette (zucchini AmE)
brunette (also *brunet* in AmE)
omelette (*omelet* AmE)
cigarette (also *cigaret* AmE)

-et derives from the French –ette
Some words are still used in modern French and we retain a similar unstressed pronunciation on the –et: *ballet, buffet, beret, cabaret,*
yet, wet, set, let, bet, get, het, jet, met, net, pet, vet, fret
basket, blanket, bracket, bucket, brisket, cricket
tablet, bullet, ballet, valet,

bonnet, cornet, cabinet   *quintet, quartet, sextet,*
claret, beret, cabaret   *cadet, bidet*
Tibet, budget, buffet   *closet, corset*
bouquet, banquet

American – *brunet, cigaret, omelet*

Common homophones list

aisle / I'll / isle
allowed / aloud
aren't / aunt
ate / eight
ball / bawl
band / banned
bare / bear
be / bee
bean / been
blew / blue
board / bored
brake / break
brews / bruise
buy / by / bye
caught / court
ceiling / sealing
cell / sell
cent / scent / sent
cereal / serial
check / cheque
chews / choose
coarse / course
cue / queue
currant / current
days / daze
dear / deer

die / dye
draft / draught
fair / fare
farther / father
find / fined
flaw / floor
flew / flu / flue
flour / flower
for / fore / four
formerly/formally
genes / jeans
grate / great
groan / grown
guessed / guest
heal / heel / he'll
hear / here
heard / herd
he'd / heed
hi / high
higher / hire
hour / our
knew / new
knot / not
know / no
knows / nose

dew / due
licence / license
loan / lone
made / maid
mail / male
mane / main
meat / meet
meter / metre
missed / mist
morning / mourning
one / won
pair / pare / pear
pause / paws / pores / pours
pawn / porn
pea / pee
peace / piece
place / plaice
plain / plane
praise / prays / preys
rain / reign / rein
raise / rays / raze
rap / wrap
raw / roar
right / rite / write
road / rode
role / roll
root / route
rose / rows
sale / sail

saw / soar / sore
scene / seen
sea / see
seam / seem
seas / sees / seize
sight / site
sew / so / sow
some / sum
son / sun
stair / stare
stationary / stationery
steal / steel
storey / story
tale / tail
there / their / they're
threw / through
throne / thrown
tide / tied
to / too / two
waist / waste
wait / weight
war / wore
weak / week
we'd / weed
weather / whether
were / where / wear
which / witch
who's / whose
wood / would
your / you're

Spelling Detective Exercise 1

Get your thinking and spelling cap on and write in the homophone for these words.

Example: 1. brews <u>bruise</u>

2. chews _____

3. claws _____

4. brows _____

5. knows _____

6. days _____

7. frays _____

8. prays _____

9. rays _____

10. pleas _____

11. teas _____

12. sighs _____

13. tacks _____

14. lacks _____

15. links _____

According to Edward Carney, some words will not provide examples in all accents.

Exercise 1 Answers

Possible answers

1. brews <u>bruise</u>
2. chews <u>choose</u>
3. claws <u>clause</u>
4. brows <u>browse</u>
5. knows <u>nose</u>
6. days <u>daze</u>
7. frays <u>phrase</u>
8. prays <u>praise</u>
9. rays <u>raise</u>
10. pleas <u>please</u>
11. teas <u>tease</u>
12. sighs <u>size</u>
13. tacks <u>tax</u>
14. lacks <u>lax</u>
15. links <u>lynx</u>

Spelling Detective Exercise 2

Get your detective hat on and think hard about which homophone goes with these past tense words.

Notice the –ed endings either have a "t" or "d" sound.

For example, *allowed* <u>*aloud*</u>   *missed* <u>*mist*</u>

1. banned _____

2. whirred _____

3. brewed _____

4. owed _____

5. mowed _____

6. bawled _____

7. swayed _____

8. missed _____

9. guessed _____

10. weighed _____

11. tacked _____

12. packed _____

13. tied _____

14. paced _____

According to Edward Carney, some words will not provide examples in all accents.

Exercise 2 Answers

1. banned <u>band</u>

2. whirred <u>word</u>

3. brewed <u>brood</u>

4. owed <u>ode</u>

5. mowed <u>mode</u>

6. bawled <u>bald</u> or <u>balled</u>

7. swayed <u>suede</u>

8. missed <u>mist</u>

9. guessed <u>guest</u>

10. weighed <u>wade</u>

11. tacked <u>tact</u>

12. packed <u>pact</u>

13. tied <u>tide</u>

14. paced <u>paste</u>

Write some memory tricks for these words.

Spelling Detective Exercise 3

Get your detective hat on again and think hard about which homophone goes with these words.

1. higher _____

2. tenner _____

3. seller _____

4. hanger _____

5. meatier _____

6. bolder _____

7. whine _____

8. whether _____

9. whale _____

10. saver _____

Spelling Detective Exercise 3 Answers

1. higher <u>hire</u>
2. tenner <u>tenor</u>
3. seller <u>cellar</u>
4. hanger <u>hangar</u>
5. meatier <u>meteor</u>
6. bolder <u>boulder</u>
7. whine <u>wine</u>
8. whether <u>weather</u>
9. whale <u>wail</u>
10. saver <u>savour / savor</u> (AmE)

Notes

Proofreading Exercise. Correct and re-write this famous poem.

The original version of this poem was written by Jerrold H. Zar in 1992. A spell checker will find little or no fault with this poem.

Eye have a spelling chequer,
It came with my Pea Sea.
It plane lee marks four my revue
Miss Steaks I can knot sea.

Eye strike the quays and type a whirred
And weight four it two say
Weather eye am write oar wrong
It tells me straight a weigh.

Eye ran this poem threw it,
My chequer tolled me sew.

_____

_____

_____

_____

_____

_____

_____

_____

Proofreading Exercise Answers

(The original version) Eye have a spelling chequer,
It came with my Pea Sea.
It plane lee marks four my revue
Miss Steaks I can knot sea.

Eye strike the quays and type a whirred
And weight four it two say
Weather eye am write oar wrong
It tells me straight a weigh.

Eye ran this poem threw it,
My chequer tolled me sew.

***

The corrected version
I have a spelling checker,
It came with my PC.
It plainly marks for my review
Mistakes I cannot see.

I strike the keys and type a word
And wait for it to say
Whether I am right or wrong
It tells me straight away.

I ran this poem through it,
My checker told me so.

Visual Spelling Patterns

Good spellers see letter patterns, links and understand relationships between words. Knowing common letter patterns is a reliable way to help spelling.

> There are some strings of letters which occur very often. Good spellers are able to remember these easily and can visualise the letter patterns in words.
> Basic Skills Agency: *Starter Pack*

> *It is only through* **visual** *familiarity with language that you can learn about the probable spelling of words. Spelling is about visual sequences of letters.*
> Sue Abell: *Helping Adults Spell*

Good spellers have an excellent visual memory for what looks right. They know the 'qua' in *qualification* is spelt with 'qua' like the other 'qua' words, such as *quarter, quantity, quaint, quality...*

They know that the suffix ending that sounds like "shun" is either: -tion, -sion or -cian. If they spell *quolificasion* like this, they can usually see that this looks wrong.

You can develop this skill, too, by practising/practicing (AmE) spelling, noticing the patterns and rules. Spelling won't happen by just reading about it - you have to work at it.

-eigh- *eight, height, weight, freight, neighbour/neighbor*
-ank- *sank, bank, thank, tank, blank, Hank*
-ink- *sink, pink, think, stink, blink, chink*
br- *brick, bridge, bright, brandy, brilliant*
gr- *green, grass, grate, great, gracious*

The pattern might make different sounds in different words. It's more about developing your visual memory for what looks right.

Identifying Letter Patterns

Letter patterns are also called letter strings.

-ight	-tch	pl-	spr-	br-	pr-
light	match	play	spring	brown	prince
bright	watch	plan	sprung	bring	princess
tight	catch	plastic	spritz	brought	print
might	hutch	plenty	sprat	brunt	price
uptight	notch	plank	sprog	Britain	prank

According to Johanna Stirling: There are certain letter patterns that occur so often that we need to be able to write them automatically as "chunks" of spelling, rather than letter-by-letter. For example:
beginning patterns: st-, br-, pl-, bl-, gl-, thr-, spr-, sk-
end patterns: -nt, -ed, -ful, -ness, -sure
vowel patterns: ou, ow, ie, ei, oy, igh, ough, au
consonant patterns: ng, th, ch, sh

It's important to start "really" seeing words, noticing patterns and thinking about words that are linked by letter pattern. Good spellers see these patterns, links, and understand relationships between words, and the exceptions.

Sounding out and visual memory

We often try and sound out an unfamiliar word to help us spell it and then use our visual memory to see if it looks right.

A lot of letter patterns can be put into sound groups, which means we can rhyme an unfamiliar word with a possible letter pattern.

So rhyming a word with another word that has the same letter pattern is a great strategy to help you recall spellings, and to see how the word might be written. But there are often exceptions that you need to learn too. Look at these they have the same patterns but with some sound exceptions:

found, pound, round but *young*
eight, weight, weigh but *height*
soon, moon, tycoon but *book, took*
because, autumn, August but *Australia*
how, now, cow but *blow, know*
match, batch, hatch but *watch*

Look at these with the same sound but different patterns, so developing your visual memory for what looks right is important.

believe, achieve but *receive*
Light, flight, right, bright slight but *write, site, kite*
air, hair, flair, affair but *hare, flare, aware, care*
plain, train, vain, rain but *plane, lane, vein, reign, champagne*

So rhyming a word can give clues or even very clear indications of likely letter patterns if we know all the possible variations.

Letter pattern dictionary and stories

To help you learn to spell these, you need to develop your visual memory for what looks right, and one strategy is to make a letter pattern dictionary and list the words by patterns, and also their sound groups. Then make letter pattern sentences or stories.

-ou- pattern

-ound- *round, pound, sound, found, hound, bound, ground, mound...* (If you have trouble spelling one on these, you can try rhyming, or use a letter pattern story rhyme: "*My hound found a round pound on the ground on top of a mound.*")

-**ouble**- *double, trouble*

-**ouple** *couple*

-**ouse** *house, mouse... "There's a mouse in my house."*

-**our** *our, scour, flour, sour, devour...* but *your, four, pour, tour...*

-**oud** *loud, proud, cloud, aloud... "He's loud and proud with his head in a cloud."*

-**out**- *out, outside, about, pout, spout, sprout...*

-**outh**- *south, mouth*

-**ount**- *count, mount, mountain, fountain...*

council, councillor/councilor (AmE)

counsellor/counselor (AmE)

Our house is your house.
young 'you' is in *young* "**You** are so **you**ng."
doubt "*It's natural to <u>be</u> in dou<u>b</u>t.*"

Notes

-ow- pattern

-ow "ow": in *how now brown cow, brow, vow, wow, allow, bow** "*How now brown cow with a big brow."*

-ow "oh": in *low, know, show, snow, grow, crow, bow*, glow, mow, stow, throw, flow, tow... "I know the snow is low but you can't mow."*

Combine them both: *"Now is the time to know how to grow and glow and vow to wow and throw those old low feelings out."*

*Can you remember **bow** from the homographs lesson? And **no** and **know** from the homophones lesson?

-own *brown, down, town, gown, clown, down, drown, frown...*
-ow *owl, fowl, growl, howl, prowl, scowl... bowl*
-ower *flower, tower, power, shower...*

-ow at the end of words:
-low *low, flow, blow, slow, below, bungalow*
-llow *willow, follow, hollow, shallow, yellow, pillow, swallow,* but *allow*
-rrow *arrow, sorrow, marrow, barrow, tomorrow*
-dow *window, shadow*

Add more words to your letter pattern dictionary when you see these patterns.

If you're not sure of the pronunciation of a word, go to www.macmillandictionary.com and www.dictionary.cambridge.org.

Let's look at the **-igh** patterns (we looked at why we have this "strange" pattern in the lesson on silent letters - can you remember?).

-igh- *high, sigh, thigh, higher*
-ight- *light, bright, delight, fight, flight, night, might, right, tight, eyesight, sightseeing...*

(But be careful; we have the same sound in **-ite** words - *bite, site, kite, write*)

-eigh- *eight, weight, weigh, neighbour/neighbor* (AmE)
but height (always write the exceptions down too)

The **-ight-** words are some of the most common words in English and trickiest to spell. We can use rhyming to help and also write sentences with the words.

Letter pattern stories
Writing sentences or drawing pictures can plant the words and pattern into your memory.

It's good to have a bright light at night or your eyesight might not be right.

My friend took a flight to New York and went sightseeing, and was delighted to see the bright lights.

Let's look at some homophone words with –ight and –ite. They have the same sound but different spelling and meaning.

write/right
*You **write words**. See the 'w' in **write words**.*
I write with my right hand. See the 'h' in right hand.

sight/site
sight, eyesight, sightseeing
building site, website, campsite
I went sightseeing but saw lots of building sites.

The long 'a' sound - "ay"

Vowel sounds can be spelled many different ways. We don't have enough vowels to cater for all the different sounds we need so we pair up the vowels. But this is not that simple because we have different patterns for the same sounds.

The same "ay" sound occurs in the -ay, -ai-, a-consonant-e patterns, and some -ey and -ei- words. But the position of the pattern in the word determines the spelling.

Many scholars didn't like the letter 'y' in the middle of root words unless they were of Greek origin, so we have the root words *pay, say, stray*, with the 'ay' pattern coming at the end of words, and the -ai- pattern in *rain, plain, drain* coming in the middle of words because the academics didn't like rayn, playn, drayn!

Magic 'e' silent 'e' at the end of words is usually used to make long vowel sounds, including the "ay" sound in *crane, plane, pane, Shane*.

We also have 'ei' making the "ay" sound, too, in *eight, neigh, weigh, weight, neighbour/neighbor, sleigh, freight, reindeer, beige*. There are only a few of these, so they can be memorized, or write a letter pattern story to help remember them:

Eight beige reindeer for my neighbour's/neighbor's sleigh were delivered by freight.

We also have 'ey' in *prey, they, hey, grey* (BrE)/gray (AmE)

We have some words where the -ai- is short and unstressed: *again, certain, said. Again* can be short or long.

More on short and long vowel sounds in the Phonic Strategies section.

Look at these

-**ay** at the end of single syllable root words	-**ai**- in the middle (never at the end)	**a_e** magic 'e' **a** + consonant(s) + e
ray	rain	crane
tray	train	trade
may	mail	male
X-ray	rail	rake
astray	available	evade
play	plain	plane
day	daily	dale
stray	strain	strange
way	wait	wave
pay	pain	pane
bay	bait	bathe
way	waist	waste
Jay	jail	Jane
stay	sail/ snail	sale / stale
say	said certain (short vowel sound)	sane

Exception: *maybe* = may + be, now a compound word from the old phrase *it may be (that)*.

Suffixes can be added to -**ay** to change the grammar, and the position! *play - plays, played, playing; say – says, saying; stay – stayed, staying, stays*, etc.

Exercise with –ain–

Write the correct words in the gaps.

Spain, certain, train, rain, sprained, complained, maintain, explain, explaining, detained, again, stained, chain, dainty

1. He fell down and _____ his ankle.

2. I'd better take an umbrella, it might _____

3. I _____ to the manager of the restaurant about the useless service.

4. I dropped a glass of red wine and _____ the carpet.

5. After the third time _____ about the loss of my gold _____ they asked me to _____ it all _____.

6. I had some cakes from the patisserie and they were so _____ and light.

7. The commuter _____ was so packed and hot, I felt dizzy and almost _____.

8. The man was _____ at customs on suspicion of smuggling.

9. I'm absolutely _____ we've met before.

10. Most people are finding it hard to _____ their standard of living.

11. She's British but she lives in _____.

Exercise Answers

Spain, certain, train, rain, sprained, fainted, complained, maintain, explain, explaining, detained, again, stained, chain, dainty

1. He fell down and <u>sprained</u> his ankle.

2. I'd better take an umbrella it might <u>rain</u>

3. I <u>complained</u> to the manager of the restaurant about the useless service.

4. I dropped a glass of red wine and <u>stained</u> the carpet.

5. After the third time <u>explaining</u> about the loss of my gold <u>chain,</u> they asked me to <u>explain</u> it all <u>again</u>.

6. I had some small cakes from the patisserie and they were so <u>dainty</u> and light.

7. The commuter <u>train</u> was so packed and hot, I felt dizzy and almost <u>fainted.</u>

8. The man was <u>detained</u> at customs on suspicion of smuggling.

9. I'm absolutely <u>certain</u> we've met before.

10. Most people are finding it hard to <u>maintain</u> their standard of living.

11. She's British but she lives in <u>Spain</u>.

Thanks to *The Spelling Pack*

Look at these patterns and the position of them in the root word

-**oy** (end)	-**oi**- (middle)
toy	toilet
boy	boil
joy / enjoy	join / joint
ploy / employ	exploit / poison
oyster* exception	choir* sound difference
-oy- is in the middle of a few words before a vowel royal / loyal foyer voyage / voyeur flamboyant	celluloid paranoid typhoid

long "oo"

-**ew**-	-**ue**-	-**ui**- middle
blew	blue	bruise
dew	due	juice
stew	sue	suit
flew	flue	fruit

"oh" sound

-**ow**- end	-**oa**- middle
low	load
tow	soap
crow	coat
grow	goal
throw	toast

B and P

If you have problems with **p** and **b**, use different coloured/colored pens and visual clues with the shape of the word.

bed looks like a bed

Common errors
think or thing

I think I understand everything now, except this thing.

-ink: *think* - to think = verb. *I think I need a drink!*
ink, think, pink, drink, rink, sink, blink, slink, brink, wink, mink...

-ing: *thing* - a thing = noun. *That ring thing is so bling.*
ping, ring, sing, bling, swing, wing, ting, zing...

than or then

It's much bigger than I thought, but then again it's cheaper than the smaller one.
than *can, tan, flan, ban, pan, bigger than. I happier than...*
then *Ken, ten, Len, Ben, pen, **then** this happened...*

Initial letters

str- *street, strip, stripe, strap, straight, strength...*
scr- *scrap, scrape, scream, scrub, scrutiny...*
spr- *spring, sprint, sprinkle, sprocket...*
sp- *spit, spot, spat, spoon, spacious*
st- *stint, stop, stunt, stance, standard*
sn- *snip, snob, snap, snatch, snoring*
sc- *scare, scale, scowl, school, scallop*
sl- *slip, slap, slob, slipper, slippery*

pl- *play, place, plate, plane/plain, plentiful*
bl- *blue, black, blow/blew, blimey*
pr- *print, prod, predict, princess, prince*
br- *bring, brand, brought, bright, brilliant*
cr- *cream, crease, crinkle, crazy, crept, crank*

Make a letter pattern dictionary and add more words and patterns.

---

brought and **bought**
Do you get these confused?
Remember: *brought* is the past of **bring**
           bought is the past tense of **buy.**

I **brought** *(bring) a cake to work that I bought at the deli.*
He bought some flowers and **brought** *(bring) them to work.*

Exercise. Write in the initial letter patterns

1. First meal of the day = ____eakfast

2. The part of the head that thinks = ____ain

3. What you need when you are thirsty = ____ink

4. It's nice on apple pie = ____eam

5. The day before Saturday = ____iday

6. When a floor is wet, it becomes ____ippery

7. This is a ____aight line

8. The past tense of *bring* is ____ought

Exercise Answers

1. First meal of the day = **breakfast**

2. The part of the head that thinks = **brain**

3. What you need when you are thirsty = **drink**

4. It's nice on apple pie = **cream**

5. The day before Saturday = **Friday**

6. When a floor is wet, it becomes **slippery**

7. This is a **straight** line ——————————————

8. The past tense of *bring* is **brought**

Write a story or sentences with as many initial letter patterns as you can.

Some "tricky" patterns

-au- pattern

"or" sound
autumn, August
Autumn comes after August.
In autumn, the leaves <u>turn</u> <u>auburn.</u>
auction, audible, authentic, author,
authorise/ authorize, authority
haul, maul, Paul
applause, cause, pause
caught, taught, daughter, naughty, slaughter, haughty

autumn
<u>Au</u>gust
bec<u>au</u>se
be<u>au</u>tiful

With *restaurant* sometimes the –au- is unstressed or silent.

***Because** you need to **always understand**.*
***B**ig **E**lephants **C**an't **A**lways **U**nderstand **S**mall **E**lephants.*

aunt, aunty, daughter, laundry, faucet (tap in BrE), sauce,
saucepan, sausage, Paul, Pauline, nauseous, nausea
caution, cautious, auto, automobile, automatic

Past tense words
(teach) *taught,* (catch*) caught*

Letter pattern stories

*I'm going for a walk with my **aunty** and **daughter** because it's a*
*beautiful **autumn** day.*
Paul, Pauline and their daughter felt nauseous after they caught
flu off their aunty.

Now write a letter pattern story sentence with –au-

Exercise with –au– word column

All the words contain the **-au-** pattern.

This helps your visual memory for what looks right.

1. A season _ _ _ _ _ _

2. The month after July _ _ _ _ _ _

3. The past tense of *teach* _ _ _ _ _ _

4. I have two children, a son and a _ _ _ _ _ _ _ _ _

5. The past tense of catch _ _ _ _ _ _

6. Another word for very pretty _ _ _ _ _ _ _ _ _ _

7. Be careful = Be _ _ _ _ _ _ _ _

8. They write books _ _ _ _ _ _ _(s)

9. To stop for a moment _ _ _ _ _

10. _ _ _ _ and _ _ _ _ _ _ _ are my uncle and

_ _ _ _ _

Exercise with –au– answers

All the words contain the **-au-** pattern.

---

1. A season   **autumn**

2. The month after July   **Autumn**

3. The past tense of *teach*   **taught**

4. I have two children, a son and a **daughter**

5. The past tense of catch   **caught**

6. Another word for very pretty   **beautiful**

7. Be careful = Be **cautious**

8. They write books   **author(s)**

9. To stop for a moment   **pause**

10. **Paul** and **Pauline** are my uncle and **aunty**

-ui- pattern
After our fruit juice, U and I need to pack our suitcases for our cruise to see the penguins.

Short sound:
build, builder, building "U and I build a house"
circuit, biscuit
guilt, guilty, guide, guild, guitar, guinea pig, guillotine, quit

Long "oo" sound: *juice, fruit, suit, suitable, suitcase, ruin, recruit, sluice, cruise, bruise*

Short Sound: *anguish, distinguish, extinguish, penguin, liquid*

Long "eye" sound:
disguise, acquire, beguile
quite, quiet
homophones: *suite / sweet*

Letter pattern stories
A penguin in a suit stopped playing his guitar and started drinking fruit juice, but the penguin ruined his suit with fruit juice.
A bruise will ruin fruit.
I quit my job because it was quite stressful, now my life is quiet.
Please keep quiet about my diet.

Now write a letter pattern story sentence with –ui-

Word column with –ui–

This helps your visual memory for what looks right.
<u>Note</u> that the same letter pattern makes different sounds.

1. The opposite of innocent _ _ _ _ _ _

2. Squeeze an orange and you get this _ _ _ _ _

3. A matching jacket and trousers _ _ _ _

4. Someone who puts up houses _ _ _ _ _ _ _

5. Apples, pears, oranges, etc. _ _ _ _ _

6. A musical instrument with strings _ _ _ _ _ _

7. To give up, stop doing something _ _ _ _

8. To carry clothes in for holidays – luggage

   _ _ _ _ _ _ _

9. Another word for silent _ _ _ _ _

10. To put out a fire, cigarette, etc.

    _ _ _ _ _ _ _ _ _

11. To destroy, damage, spoil something _ _ _ _

12. To go on holiday and travel around on a ship

    _ _ _ _ _ _

Word column answers

1. **guilty** The opposite of innocent

2. **juice** Squeeze an orange and you get this

3. **suit** A matching jacket and trousers

4. **builder** Someone who puts up houses

5. **fruit** Apples, pears, oranges, etc.

6. **guitar** A musical instrument with strings

7. **quit** To give up, stop doing something

8. **suitcase** To carry clothes in for holidays - luggage

9. **quiet** Another word for silent

10. **extinguish** To put out a fire, cigarette, etc.

11. **ruin** To destroy, damage, spoil something

12. **cruise** To go on holiday and travel around on a ship.

-ea-

There are 8 sounds for -ea-

*I **hear** that an **early breakfast** of beautiful **peaches, pears** and **steak** is good for your **health** and **heart**.*

long e "ee": *sea, pea, tea, eat, meat, beat, heat, neat, seat, treat, breathe, clean, lean, mean, bean, bead, read, knead, plead, lead, seam, team, beam, steam, dream, cream, scream, stream, jeans, beak, leak, weak, peak, sneak, creak, squeak, heal, real, really, deal, meal, seal, steal, squeal, each, beach, peach, teach, reach, east, feast, beast, peace, tease, please, easy, season, leaf, leaves...*

short e: *head, bread, dead, tread, spread, death, breath, dread, deaf, wealth, health, read (past tense), lead (metal), breakfast, breath, sweat, ready, heavy, heaven, weather...*

long u "who": *beauty, beautiful, beautician...*

long "ear": *ear, near, hear, dear, year, fear, tear (cry), clear, beard, gear, smear, idea...*

long a sound "ay": *break, steak, great*. These 3 are the only common words with this sound.

r influenced long sounds
long "ar": *heart, hearth, hearty, heartfelt...*
long "er": *wear, bear, swear, pear, tear (rip)...*
long "ur": *early, earth, heard, learn, earn, search, pearl, rehearse, rehearsal, yearn...*

Exercise

1. Summer, autumn, winter, spring are _____.

2. British people are obsessed with the _____ and always carry an umbrella with them.

3. My _____ is very good; I never go to the doctor's.

4. Google is a _____ engine.

Exercise Answers

1. Summer, autumn, winter, spring are <u>seasons</u>.

2. British people are obsessed with the <u>weather</u> and always carry an umbrella with them.

3. My <u>health</u> is very good; I never go to the doctor's.

4. Google is a <u>search</u> engine.

Word column exercise with –ea–

1. We live on planet _ _ _ _ _

2. The past tense of *hear* _ _ _ _ _

3. When something or someone is very pretty

   _ _ _ _ _ _ _ _ _

4. This person's job is in a classroom _ _ _ _ _ _ _

5. The points of a compass are north, _ _ _ _ _, south and west.

6. 12 months = a _ _ _ _

7. To have lots of money means you're _ _ _ _ _ _ _

8. The opposite of strong is _ _ _ _

9. This is the first *meal* of the day _ _ _ _ _ _ _ _ _

10. The plural of *leaf* is _ _ _ _ _ _

11. Another word for *perspire* is _ _ _ _ _

12. You _ _ _ _ _ clothes, you _ _ _ food, you _ _ _ _ books.

Word column exercise answers

1. We live on planet <u>earth</u>

2. The past tense of *hear* <u>heard</u>

3. When something or someone is very pretty <u>beautiful</u>

4. This person's job is in a classroom <u>teacher</u>

5. The points of a compass are north, <u>east</u>, south and west.

6. 12 months = a <u>year</u>

7. To have lots of money means you're <u>wealthy</u>

8. The opposite of strong is <u>weak</u>

9. This is the first *meal* of the day <u>breakfast</u>

10. The plural of *leaf* is <u>leaves</u>

11. Another word for *perspire* is <u>sweat</u>

12. You <u>wear</u> clothes, you <u>eat</u> food, you <u>read</u> books.

Write a letter pattern story or 3 sentences with as many -ea- words as you can.

-ea- word search

```
e u b y q z i l e a r n k t c r n d
d o g s s k b f r g r e f a e n t t
n z p h g a t a n r d d a h e n u a
p s i b e a e y c n q n c l t t b e
b d g r j a e t d j k a e t l n s r
w r i e a a v r w s e h q j e y k g
j e h h r m a y n t s e a s o n b c
a a l t c e l a e m c j y k x s e r
t m h a h f c x g g s y r o k h a s
n s n e c w t r a e h m r z k k u h
w s a w d c t b i k t c f c p t v
i z q f r a k i i c s s d y s q y a
r o b e k i i g k a b y x z f l s t
j x a a i a p v r g c l p g z f d q
m m l s e z e m z m z w v f q y v q
y m f u a w l r j u f q g s y c c x
q t f j w j u t b p o e b s k n t q
y v z o l y k n f x u z l s d q o g
```

beauty
breakfast
cream
dream
earth
easy
great
heard
heart
heavy
learn
meal
really
season
steak
teacher
weather

-ate

ate, hate, fate, gate, date, mate, plate, skate, state, later, relate, migrate, sedate, cheapskate, inflate, aggravate, concentrate, illustrate, translate, certificate, chocolate, climate, deliberate, delicate, immediately, desperate, unfortunate, exhilarate, intimidate, sophisticated, accommodate, demonstrate, exaggerate...

Look at the following words. They are stress shift words, which means that they change stress and sound slightly differently depending on how we use the word.

Read this sentence: *It's hard to **separate** the **separate** bits.*

Notice how the -ate in "to **separate**" (verb) is more stressed than "the **separate** bits" (noun).

to "sep" "a" "RATE" stressed (verb) *Can you separate them?*
"SEP" "rut" unstressed (adjective) *It's a separate word.*

alternate (verb) / (adjective)
moderate (verb) / (adjective)
deliberate (verb) / (adjective)
estimate (verb) / (noun)
elaborate (verb) / (adjective)
graduate (verb) / (noun)
associate (verb) / (noun)
delegate (verb) / (noun)
certificate (verb) / (noun)

Knowing these stress shift words can help you with the spelling of them, especially the letter before the -ate.

Say the long verb versions slowly and exaggeratedly:
"e" "lab" "o" "rate" vs. "e" "lab" "rut"
"sep" "a" "rate" vs. "sep" "rut"

Write a letter pattern story or 3 sentences,
for example, *I ate some delicate chocolate with my mate.*

Word Column
All the words contain the **-ate-** pattern

1. The past tense of eat _ _ _

2. This is sweet and comes in dark or milk
   _ _ _ _ _ _ _ _ _

3. June 4th; 20th Feb; Wed, 6th May are all _ _ _ _ _

4. Another word for a friend _ _ _ _

5. To give a rough value, amount, and price of something
   The builder gave me an _ _ _ _ _ _ _ _ *for the work.*

6. To say something is bigger, better, worse than it is
   _ _ _ _ _ _ _ _ _

7. To really focus on something and not get distracted
   _ _ _ _ _ _ _ _ _ _ _

8. Instant. Sudden. Occurring now.
   Take _ _ _ _ _ _ _ _ _ *action.*

Word Column Answers

All the words contain the **-ate-** pattern

1. The past tense of eat <u>ate</u>

2. This is sweet and comes in dark or milk <u>chocolate</u>

3. June 4th; 20th Feb; Wed, 6th May are all <u>dates</u>

4. Another word for a friend <u>mate</u>

5. To give a rough value, amount, and price of something
   The builder gave me an <u>estimate</u> for the work.

6. To say something is bigger, better, worse than it is
   <u>exaggerate</u>

7. To really focus on something and not get distracted
   <u>concentrate</u>

8. Instant. Sudden. Occurring now.
   Take <u>immediate</u> action.

Next, we're looking at –ant or –ent.

Can you see which is correct?

important or importent?
restaurant or restaurent?
independant or independent?

Check your answers on the next page.

130

-ant/-ent, -antly/-ently, -ance/-ence, -ancy/-ency

These are tricky patterns because they sound alike.

Let's use an *ant* and a *tent* as a mnemonic/memory trick.

ant	ent

This **ant** is eleg**ant** and pleas**ant** but not arrog**ant** or irrelev**ant**. Adam Ant was a pop star in the 80s. (Notice the play on the word *adamant*.)	Stud**ents** are cont**ent** to sleep in t**ents** to be independ**ent** and differ**ent**.

-tant	**-tent**
assistant, important, distant, instant, hesitant, reluctant	content, competent, consistent, persistent

-rant	**-rent**
fragrant, ignorant, restaurant, warrant, vagrant	parent, apparent, tyrant, different, current

-dant	**-dent**
abundant, redundant, attendant, descendant	resident, president, student, accident, evident, independent

-lant	**-lent**
jubilant, stimulant, plant, transplant	silent, violent, equivalent, excellent, repellent

-cant	**-cent**
vacant, scant, significant recent	cent, accent, scent, decent, innocent

Which **ant** are you?

*ele**gant**, important, plea**sant**, toler**ant**, vibrant, exuberant,
observant, gallant, relevant, extravagant, brilliant, vigilant,
abundant, jubilant, exuberant, ench**ant**ed, constant, valiant,
observant, triumphant*
or
*distant, dominant, arrogant, vacant, flippant, hesitant,
ignorant, reluctant, irrelevant, resistant, defiant, repugnant,
stagnant, nonchalant?*

Are you *pregnant, an accountant, a tenant, an elephant,
a consonant, an immigrant, a restaurant, a giant, a
contestant,
a tyrant, an infant, a plant, a fragrant vagrant, an assistant,
redundant?*

Can you think of a memory trick for these? Or, break them
into syllables or words within words and then write 3
sentences.

132

Notice these patterns:

-ant	-antly	-ance	-ancy
arrogant	arrogantly	arrogance	--
relevant	relevantly	relevance	relevancy
irrelevant	irrelevantly	irrelevance	irrelevancy
elegant	elegantly	elegance	--
abundant	abundantly	abundance	--
tolerant	tolerantly	tolerance	--
tenant	--	--	tenancy
vacant	vacantly	--	vacancy
dominant	dominantly	dominance	--
hesitant	hesitantly	--	hesitancy
significant	significantly	significance	--
extravagant	extravagantly	extravagance	--

We have some root words that just add the –ance ending, or drop the 'e' and add -ance:

perform – *performance*
avoid – *avoidance*
appear – appearance
annoy – *annoyance*
inherit – *inheritance*
insure – *insurance*
guide – *guidance*
account – accountant, accountancy
observe – *observant, observance*
ignore – *ignorant, ignorance*

-ant and –ance / -ancy are used with hard 'c' and 'g' sounds
elegant/*elegance*, extravagant/*extravagance*,
significant/*significance*   vacant – vacate – vacancy

How differ**ent** are you?

*confid**ent**, excellent, magnificent, independ**ent**, intelligent,
eloquent, silent, innocent, different, competent, resilient,
patient, efficient, decent, persistent, talented, consistent,
prudent,*

or

*violent, decadent, disobedient, complacent, impatient,
insolent?*

Are you *a resident, a correspondent, a patient, a client, a
parent, a gent, an agent, an adolescent?*

Can you think of a memory trick for these? Write some
sentences.

I **reside** here so I'm a **resid**ent in this **reside**nce.

Who's resid**ent** in the **tent**?
The gent in the tent is a permanent resident.

-ent	-ently	-ence	-ency
different	differently	difference	--
resident	--	residence	residency
independent	independently	independence	codependency
efficient	efficiently	--	efficiency
silent	silently	silence	--
innocent	innocently	innocence	--
excellent	excellently	excellence	excellency
permanent	permanently	permanence	permanency

-ment is a very popular suffix added to root words to form nouns to refer to a result of an action or process: *excitement, curtailment*, disappointment. Some of them are in the commonly misspelled list: *argument, embarrassment, equipment, government, environment, harassment, parliament.*

Also: *management, apartment, assessment, comment, compartment, document, entertainment, experiment, development, commitment, payment, employment, unemployment, sentiment, statement, supplement, torment, settlement, instrument...*

Keep the 'e' in
excitement, arrangement, advertisement, achievement, involvement, replacement, endorsement, management, pavement...

Exceptions: But drop the 'e' in argue + ment = *argument*. Can you remember the memory trick?

acknowledgement or *acknowledgment* are both acceptable but *acknowledgment* is chiefly used in American English.

Oxford Dictionary says: *In British English, the normal spelling in general contexts is **judgement**. However, the spelling **judgment** is conventional in legal contexts, and in American English.*

-ere to -rence / -rent
revere – reverence / reverent
adhere – adherence / adherent
cohere – coherence / coherent
interfere – interference

Exception: persevere – *perseverance*

er + ence = -rence
confer – conf**erence**
infer – *inference*
prefer – *preference*
refer – *reference*
transfer – *transference*
differ – *difference*

If the stem word ends in a soft 'c' and 'g' then the ending will be –ence or –ency.
adolescent - adolescence, indulgent – indulgence,
urgent – urgency, complacent – complacency
agent – agency, emergency, decent – decency,
belligerent – belligerence – belligerency
proficient - proficiency
innocent – innocence, negligent – negligence
intelligent – intelligence, efficient - efficiency

Exception: **vengeance**

If a word contains **-cid-, -fid-, -sid- or -vid-** before the ending, use the **-ence** suffix: *confidence, evidence, incidence, residence, providence.*

Warning
You don't need to know or remember these rules, just take note of the patterns, but now at least you know why the spelling is the way it is. And some of the words are useful to know.

-ent word search

Word searches are good for developing your visual memory.

```
a t m p o y t g t c i t i r t
t z n c a n r n p n i n t e n
k n h e e r e o d q n e t c e
t i e d l n e e g o t l t e l
h n u u i l p n c q e o n n a
p t e t q e e e t b l i e t t
s j n l n e n c g l l v n e s
c o i d i t r u x g i w a f x
c l e b g s q f u e g y m f g
y n t n e t s i s r e p r i j
t c o n f i d e n t n x e c o
w t n e g r u g q n t v p i e
t w v d z b x i q r n c k e d
t n e d i c c a a n c i e n t
v j m r l d o m c i r e d t y
```

accident
ancient
confident
continent
efficient
excellent
frequent
independent
innocent
intelligent
parent
permanent
persistent

recent
silent
student
talent
urgent
violent

Exercise. Write in the **ent** or **ant** ending.

independ_____

assist_____

suffici_____

anci_____

import_____

perman_____

restaur_____

arrog_____

pregn_____

ineffici_____

abund_____

pleas_____

tal_____

viol_____

differ_____

confid_____

import_____

relev_____

Exercise answers

independent   (see all those e's)

assistant

sufficient

ancient

important

permanent

restaurant

arrogant

pregnant

inefficient

abundant

pleasant

talent

violent

different

confident

important

relevant

Notes

139

Exercise. Write in the **ance** or **ence** ending.

independ_____

assist_____

arrog_____

import_____

perman_____

abund_____

sent_____

viol_____

experi_____

differ_____

confid_____

relev_____

Exercise answers

independence

assistance

arrogance

importance

permanence

abundance

sentence

violence

experience

difference

confidence

relevance

Notes

Word Families

Word families and visual links/patterns between words can help with spelling and help us understand why we have some "strange" spellings.

> *These relationships in spelling help us to understand the meaning of words much more than the pronunciation does.* Noam Chomsky

> *The purpose of English spelling isn't about the sound but the visual links between words.* Vivian Cook

> *English spelling is often for the eye rather than the ear, and focussing on visual links can help us work out difficult words like homophones, silent letters and word order, like 'two' and 'light'.* Johanna Stirling

Let's have a look at some word families, and how they're linked by letter pattern and meaning.

-sign- from Latin *signum* "to mark, indicate, a symbol"
sign, signal, signpost, signature, design, resignation...

Thanks to Johanna Sterling's book Teaching Spelling

142

> Although many times the spelling of a word may appear odd, an understanding of its origin can provide the most powerful key to remembering the spelling.
>
> Bear, Invernizzi, Templeton, Johnston: *Words Their Way.*

-ped- -ject- -tract- -struct-
Which of these patterns means **build**?
Which of these means to **pull**?
Which means to **throw**?
Which means **foot**?
Read on and find out.

-terr- from Latin *terra* for "earth, land, ground"
terrain, territory, subterranean, Mediterranean, extraterrestrial, terrestrial, terrace, terra cotta, terra firma, terrier (a dog that digs in the earth!)

-rupt- from Latin for "broken"
rupture, interrupt, disrupt, disruption, erupt, eruption, bankrupt, corrupt, abrupt...

-mal- from Latin for "bad"
malfunction, malpractice, malnourished, malady, malignant, malaria, malcontent, malicious, malign, maladjusted, malevolent...

Some common words with the –ct- pattern

-ject- from Latin "throw"
reject (throw away!), *rejection, eject, projectile, trajectory, projection* (to throw light on something!), *dejection, object, objection, trajectory, adjective* (to throw light on nouns!)...

-struct- Latin for "build"
structure, construction, constructive, instruct, instruction, destruct, destruction, reconstruction, obstruct...

-spect- Latin for "see/look"
inspect, inspector, inspection, spectator, spectacle, spectacles, aspect, spectacular, respect, circumspect, introspection, retrospective, speculate...

-junct- from Latin for "join"
(Tricky pattern so remember the **j** and **n** in the meaning to **join**)
junction, juncture, conjunction, injunction, adjunct, disjunction...

-duct-/-duc- Latin for "lead"
conductor, introduction, educate, induct, induction, viaduct, aqueduct, deduct, reproduce, reduce, duct, abduct...

-sect-/-seg- Latin for "cut"
section, sector, segment, intersect, bisect, dissect, insect...

-tract- means to *pull or draw out, pull out*. We can see from the other members of this word family, they are all to do with pull in some way.

abstract
attract
attracted
attracting
attraction
attractive
contract
contracted
contractor
contraction
contractual
detract

detracting
detraction
detractor
distract
distracted
distraction
distractions
extract
extracted
extraction

protract
protracted
retract
retractable
retracted
retracting
retraction
retracts
subcontract
subcontracted
subcontracting
subcontractor
subtract
subtracted
subtraction
subtracting
tract
traction
tractor
unattractive

-miss-/-mit- Latin for "send"
(Helps you remember the double 's')
trans**mit**/trans**miss**ion, omit/omission submit/*submission*,
dismissal, permission, mission, missile, emission, promise

-val- from Latin *valere* related to "worth or strength"
value, equivalent, interval, evaluate, valuation, devalue...

145

-ary/-ery/-ory

These endings are tricky because they sound the same. They all come from Latin for "belonging to", "connected with", "having to do with (whatever it is affixed to)": *library, machinery, victory*

-ary

library (connected with books), *missionary* (belonging to a mission), *revolutionary, stationary* (originally meant belonging to a military station), *primary* (from Latin first), *dictionary* (manual or book of words), *vocabulary* (list of words)

Letter pattern endings: *–sary, -nary, -rary, -lary, -mary, -tary*

neces**sary**, anniversary, glossary, tempo**rary**, library, literary
extraordi**nary**, imaginary, stationary, dictionary, ordinary, missionary, revolutionary, legen**dary**, boundary
custo**mary**, primary, summary, infirmary
documen**tary**, secretary, hereditary, military, solitary, elementary
vocabu**lary**, salary, burglary, diary, auxiliary

Plural spelling rule - to *make plurals change the y to –ies*
*library – libraries, dictionary – dictionaries, diary – diaries
summary – summaries, documentary - documentaries
burglary – burglaries, revolutionary - revolutionaries
secretaries, missionaries, primaries, salaries*

Write –ary sentences or stories

146

-ery

cemetery ce me te ry
See all the e's: *A cemetery is **ee**rie with lots of greenery.*

***very**, every, discovery, bravery, shivery, slavery*
*bat**tery**, mystery, artery, lottery, blustery, adultery,*
*dysentery, monastery, flattery, watery, pottery, rob**bery**,*
*bribery, snobbery,   ima**gery**, surgery, forgery, nur**sery**,*
*misery, gro**cery**, confectio**nery**, sce**nery**, stationery,*
*machinery, vinery, **celery**, gallery, peri**phery**, treachery,*
*feathery, coo**kery**, bakery*

Notice how a lot of these words are formed:
confection – confectioner – *confectionery*

cook – coo**ker** – *cookery*	bake – baker – *bakery*
rob – robber – *robbery*	brave – braver – *bravery*
bribe – briber - *bribery*	brew – brewer - *brewery*
image – *ima**gery***	flatter – *flattery*
slave – *slavery*	stationer – *stationery*
scene – *scenery*	silver – *silvery*
machine – *machinery*	summer – *summery*
nurse – *nursery*	water – *watery*
forge – *forgery*	recover – *recovery*

British vs. American
jewellery vs. *jewelry*

Plurals – again change the y to ies
*battery – batt**eries**   mystery – myst**eries***
*forg**eries**   stationeries   discoveries   breweries*
nurseries   groceries   surgeries   bakeries

> Write an –ery/-eries pattern story with as many words as
> you can.

-ory
ca*tegory*, allegory,
lava*tory*, satisfactory, derogatory, promontory, inventory,
laboratory, depository, inflammatory, directory,
conservatory, mandatory, contradictory, explanatory,
factory, territory, history, victory, predatory, dormitory,
laboratory, exploratory
acce*ssory*, derisory, advisory, sensory, cursory, compulsory
memory, theory, ivory, story

Notice how some of these words are formed

contributor – *contributory*   inventor - *inventory*
director - *directory*   victor – *victory*
predator - *predatory*   advisor – *advisory*
sensor – *sensory*   auditor – *auditory*
supervisor – *supervisory*   respirator – *respiratory*

A lot of the words are linked to the **-tion** pattern

satisfaction – *satisfactory*   preparation – *preparatory*
invention – *inventory*   exploration – *exploratory*
sensation – *sensory*   explanation - *explanatory*
conservation – *conservatory*   inflammation – *inflammatory*
direction – *directory*   circulation – *circulatory*

Plurals - change the y to ies
directory – *direct**ories***   memory – *mem**ories***
stories, theories, accessories, laboratories, victories...

Write an –ory/-ories story
This story is about a theory...

-mem- from Latin for "memory, mindful"
remember, memory, memorise/memorize, memorial, memorandum, memento, memorabilia, commemorate...

-path- from Greek for "feeling, suffer"
sympathy, sympathetic, sympathise/sympathize, pathos
empathy (with feeling), *empathise/empathize,*
apathy (without feeling), *apathetic, antipathy, pathetic*

-phon- from Greek for "sound"
phone, telephone, headphones,
microphone, xylophone, symphony
homophone, phonics, phoneme

-ous from Latin meaning "full of", "of the nature of"

glorious – full of glory   *furious* – full of fury
dangerous – full of danger   *mysterious* – full of mystery

mountainous, laborious, notorious, glamorous, famous, infamous, jealous, enormous, ridiculous, stupendous, curious...

Notice in British English, when we add the -ous, -ious to words ending in -our, we drop the 'u' in it: glamo<u>u</u>r – *glam<u>o</u>rous*, humour – *humorous*, vigour – *vigorous*, rigour – *rigorous*, labour – *laborious*...

-eous
gorgeous, advantageous, courageous, outrageous - keep the 'e' to retain the soft "g" and "c" sounds

Also: courteous, miscellaneous, nauseous, hideous, spontaneous...

-uous (the "you" sound helps)
strenuous, continuous, ambiguous, conspicuous, contemptuous, voluptuous, vacuous...

Change the y to i + ous = **-ious**
glory – *glorious*, fury – *furious*, vary – *various*, envy – *envious*, luxury – *luxurious*, harmony – *harmonious*, study – *studious*.
Also: *serious, bilious, curious, notorious, previous...*

"shus" sound in 'ci' + ous = **-cious**: *vicious, conscious, precious, delicious, gracious, spacious...*
Also "sh" sound in –xious *anxious*

Change the **f** to **v** + ous = **-vous**
grief – *grievous*, mischief - *mischievous*

Exercise
What do you think these mean in Latin?

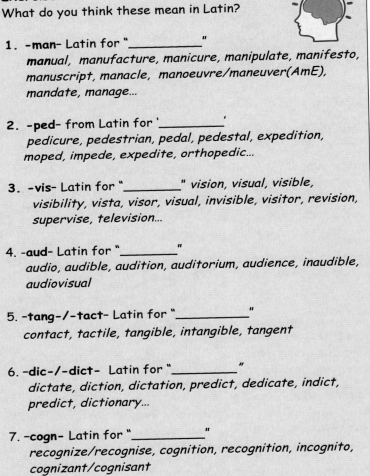

1. **-man-** Latin for "_____"
manual, manufacture, manicure, manipulate, manifesto, manuscript, manacle, manoeuvre/maneuver(AmE), mandate, manage...

2. **-ped-** from Latin for '_____'
pedicure, pedestrian, pedal, pedestal, expedition, moped, impede, expedite, orthopedic...

3. **-vis-** Latin for "_____" vision, visual, visible, visibility, vista, visor, visual, invisible, visitor, revision, supervise, television...

4. **-aud-** Latin for "_____"
audio, audible, audition, auditorium, audience, inaudible, audiovisual

5. **-tang-/-tact-** Latin for "_____"
contact, tactile, tangible, intangible, tangent

6. **-dic-/-dict-** Latin for "_____"
dictate, diction, dictation, predict, dedicate, indict, predict, dictionary...

7. **-cogn-** Latin for "_____"
recognize/recognise, cognition, recognition, incognito, cognizant/cognisant

Exercise answers

1. **-man**– Latin for "hand"
   manual (working with your hands) *manufacture, manicure, manipulate, manifesto, manuscript, manacle, mandate, manage, manoeuvre/maneuver(AmE)...*

2. **-ped**– from Latin for "foot"
   pedicure, pedestrian, pedal, pedestal, expedition, moped, impede, expedite, orthopedic...

3. **-vis**– Latin for "seeing/vision"
   vision, visual, visible, visibility, vista, visor, visual, invisible, visitor, revision, supervise, television...

4. **-aud** – Latin for "hear"   *audio, audible, audition, auditorium, audience, inaudible, audiovisual*

5. **tang/tact** – Latin for "touch"
   contact, tactile, tangible, intangible, tangent

6. **-dic-/-dict-** Latin for "speak"
   dictate, diction, dictation, predict, dedicate, indict, predict, dictionary...

7. **-cogn**- Latin for "know"
   recognize/recognise, cognition, recognition, incognito, cognizant/cognisant

Exercise

Can you remember what these Latin stem words/patterns mean?

Write in four words that belong to the pattern.

-**val**-

-**ject**-

-**terr**-

-**man**-

-**tract**-

-**mal**-

-**vis**-

Next we're going to look at the numbers 'one' and 'two'

Why is there a 'w' in *two* and a "w" sound in *one*?

153

Two

Word families and visual links between words are very important to help us with spelling and understanding the meaning of words. They also help us understand why we have some "strange" patterns, like the 'tw' in *two* and the 'on' pattern in *one* and *once*.

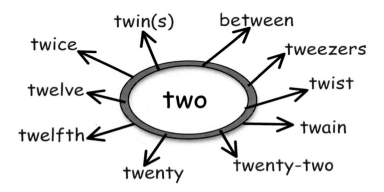

Notice they're all related to **two** in some way. *Twice, twelve* and *twenty* are obvious. *Twins* (two things alike), *between* (between two things), *tweezers* (two pieces of metal), *twist* (two things together). But the 'tw' is pronounced differently in *two*. Why?

In Old English/Anglo-Saxon, they had 'w' in the spelling *twā* and most likely pronounced it similar to the Dutch *twee*, and German *zwei*. Then it became silent, but left in the spelling to show the history of the word.

Twain = Old English *twegen*, masculine of *twā*
The comment **never the twain shall meet**, suggesting that **two things** are too different to exist alongside each other.
oxforddictionaries.com

One

one – *once* – *only* – *none* – *alone* - *lonely* are all related to *one* in some way. But *one* and *once* are pronounced differently.

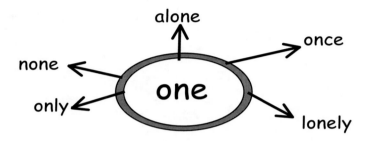

The 'w' sound was added to *one* and *once* in popular speech somewhere between 1150-1476, and became standard in the 17th century. We don't know why it happened. Pronunciation is always changing to make speaking/pronunciation easier, but the spelling remains fixed.

Remember the letter 'c' (not 's') in *once, twice, thrice*.

lone + ly = *lonely*
loneliness = lone + ly = *lonely* then change the 'y' to 'i' with ness = *loneliness*

Take note: *alone* is spelled as one word.

Building Words With Prefixes and Suffixes

Uncomfortably, disinterested, unmanageable, indifferently,
unnecessarily, anticlockwise, misrepresentation...
Do long words scare you?

These "long" words aren't so scary and difficult to learn if
you know how they break down into manageable bits called
root words, prefixes and *suffixes*. Understanding how words
are built with these is an important spelling strategy.

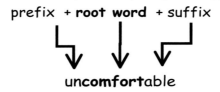

In the section on Spelling Systems, we saw how we can
alter/"morph" words with prefixes and suffixes (the
Morphological System). This also involves spelling rules (The
Graphemic System), and the history of spelling (The
Etymological System).

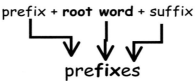

prefixes *morphs* down into: **pre + fix + es** which is added to
words ending in *x, z, s, sh, ch* to form plurals (spelling rule).
More on suffix spelling rules later.

The Oxford Dictionaries Online says: Some prefixes and
suffixes are part of our living language, in that people
regularly use them to create new words for modern
products, concepts or situations. For example:
security – *biosecurity*, clutter – *declutter*,
space – *cyberspace*, media – *multimedia*, email – *emailer*

Prefixes are added straight onto the root word:
trust/mistrust, sure/unsure, patient/impatient

Suffixes sometimes change the root word:
fit/fits/fitter/fitness, happy/happily/happiness

We can create **word families** by adding prefixes and suffixes:

certain – uncertain, certainty, certainly, uncertainly
believe – believable, unbelievable, believing, believed
manage – manager, manageress, managed, managing, manageable, unmanageable, management
employ – employed, employee, employer, employment, unemployed, employability
know – knowledge, knowledgeable, acknowledge, acknowledging, acknowledgement(s), unacknowledged
represent – represents, represented, representing, representative, representatively, unrepresentative, representation, misrepresent, representations, misrepresenting, misrepresentation, representational

---

So knowing how words are built with prefixes and suffixes can help you spell "long" words, and helps you not be so scared of them.

According to Sue Abell, you need to understand and to **see** that often the longest words are potentially the easiest to learn.

You need to understand that each part of the word carries meaning. In each word, there is a core element of meaning, which is the root of the word.

You can improve your spelling, increase your knowledge of words and spellings, and dramatically improve your confidence with spelling if you understand that long words are often made up of a "root" word plus "bits" added to the beginning and/or end (these "bits" are called prefixes and suffixes).   Basic Skills Agency

Prefixes

unhappy, unnecessary, immature, inappropriate, empower, multinational, superstore, transatlantic, prearranged...

Prefixes are little words we add to the beginning of root words to make the word negative or the opposite meaning.

There are hundreds of prefixes. Some of the most popular are: **in-, ir-, il-, im-, un-, dis-, pre-, ex-, anti-, uni-**

The most common prefixes are **un-, re-, in-, dis-**

un + *happy* = **unhappy** = not happy = sad
re + paint = **repaint** = paint again
under + cooked = **undercooked** = not cooked enough
un + *comfortable* = **uncomfortable** = not comfortable
in + *correct* = **incorrect** = wrong = not correct, not right
dis + *like* = **dislike** = don't like
il + legal = **illegal** = not legal
im + patient = **impatient** = not patient
un + usual = **unusual** = not usual
in + correct = **incorrect** = not correct or wrong or not right
dis + satisfied = **dissatisfied** = not happy, not good, not as good
in + complete = **incomplete** = not complete

Notice how they can enhance your vocabulary and give you a massive choice of words. Choose wisely because adding some prefixes can make the word more formal or academic, and not appropriate for informal emails to family or friends! Look at the examples below.

*I am **dissatisfied** with the service I received on Saturday* (formal letter of complaint).
*I'm **unhappy** with the service I got on Saturday* (informal email to a friend).
*That's **wrong**! That's **incorrect**!*

Notice the double letters in the following words. We add the prefix to the root word so we get double letters:

dis + satisfied = dis**s**atisfied	mis + spell = mi**ss**pell
un + necessary = un**n**ecessary	im + mature = i**mm**ature
ir + responsible = i**rr**esponsible	il + legal = i**ll**egal

Prefix rules

Can you see the rules in these words?
illogical, illegal, illegible
irregular, irresponsible, irresistible
immature, immortal, immigrant
impossible, imperfect, impatient

There are plenty of exceptions to these rules, but the pronunciation can help. Historically, some prefixes were changed to aid speaking and pronunciation.

Prefix rules and exceptions

Use 'il' before words starting with 'l'
legible – *illegible, illegal, illuminate, illiterate, illogical*
illegally (so many l's) = il + legal + ly
(But *unlawful, unlearn, unless...* 'un' helps the pronunciation)

Use 'ir' before words starting with 'r'
relevant – *irrelevant, irreconcilable, irregular, irradiate, irresistible irrelevantly* = ir + relevant + ly
(But *unreal, unrated...* 'un' helps the pronunciation)

Use 'im' before words stating with 'm', 'p' 'b'
mature – *immature, immigrant, immortal, immaculate,*
possible – *impossible*, perfect – *imperfect, impair, impact*
(But *unpack, unpick, unpaid... unmarked, unmarried...*)

balance – *imbalance, imbecile, imbibe, imbue*
(But *inbox, inbound, inbuilt...*)

Prefix Exercise 1

Make these into the opposite meaning by using a prefix:

1. sure   _____

2. patient   _____

3. able   _____

4. certain   _____

5. sense   _____

6. legal   _____

7. logical   _____

8. responsible   _____

9. shape   _____

10. natural   _____

11. spell   _____

12. necessary   _____

Prefix Exercise 1. Answers

1. sure ➜ <u>unsure</u>

2. patient ➜ <u>impatient</u>

3. able ➜ <u>unable</u>

4. certain ➜ <u>uncertain</u>

5. sense ➜ <u>nonsense</u>

6. legal ➜ <u>illegal</u>

7. logical ➜ <u>illogical</u>

8. responsible ➜ <u>irresponsible</u>

9. shape ➜ <u>misshape</u>

10. natural ➜ <u>unnatural</u>

11. spell ➜ <u>misspell</u>

12. necessary ➜ <u>unnecessary</u>

Notes

Common prefixes with their meanings (some mean different things with different words).

un, in, il, im, ir, dis, non
These make nouns, verbs, adjectives into the negative, opposite meaning and mean "not".
unfair, untidy = not fair, not tidy
incomplete, informal, illegal, illegitimate,
immature, impatient, irregular, irrational,
dishonest, dislike, non-smoker, non-toxic...

de, dis, un, re
These indicate reversal of a verb's actions - reverse, back, again.
defrost, debug, detach...
untie, unwrap, undo...
repaint, retry, redo, return, retell, regain...
disconnect, discontinue, disable...

over, under, sub, mis
These indicate something is wrong, bad, under, lowly or excessive.
oversleep (too much sleep), *overpopulated* (too many people, excessive)
undervalued (not valued enough), *undercooked* (not cooked enough)
substandard, subspecies, subservient...
misunderstand, miscalculate, misinterpreted, misinformed...

hyper, mega, super, ultra, micro, mini
These indicate size: very big, very small, too much.
hypermarket, hyperactive, hyperbolic...
megastore, megabyte, megabucks...
supermarket, supermodel, supertanker...
ultrasound, ultra-modern, ultraviolet...
microwave, microchip, microbrewery...
miniskirt, minibus, miniseries...

mono, uni, bi, tri, multi, semi
These indicate number, frequency, shape.
monorail, monologue = one
universal, unisex = one, or the same
bilingual, bicycle = two
triangle, tripod = three
semicircle, semicolon = half
multinational, multi-storey/multistorey = many

Hyphens (-) (Taken from my Punctuation Guide & Workbook)

e-book or ebook, e-mail or email, multi-storey or multistorey, anticlockwise or anti-clockwise?
Which is right?

Both are right. Use a good dictionary to check the latest spellings with hyphens.

Hyphens come and go. When it's a new word, it usually starts with a hyphen so as not to confuse people, then soon the hyphen is dropped (*e-mail* is now *email*). This has been going on for centuries!

You must use a hyphen when the prefix comes before a capital letter, *anti-British, pro-European*, because a capital letter can't appear inside a word ~~proEuropean~~.
mid-July, pro-European, post-Vietnam, un-American, pro-Canadian, anti-Reagan, off-Broadway, ex-Foreign Secretary...

Prefixes such as re-, co-, pre, anti-, self- sometimes have hyphens when added to words, sometimes they don't.

co-owner/coexist
pre-war/preview
anti-hero/antibiotic
self-assured/selfsame
up-market/upbeat

For single letter prefixes, most have hyphens:
*X-ray, X-rated, X-certificate, U-turn, A-list, T-shirt,
T-bone, Y-chromosome, T-junction/T-intersection...*
Notice the single letter is a capital.

But these newer, internet-related words have lowercase single letters. The 'e' stands for *electronic*:
e-book/ebook, e-mail/email, e-commerce, e-cash (the hyphen will probably be dropped soon).

If a word looks the same as another, we need the hyphen:
recover/re-cover – I have *recovered* from my illness.
> I have *re-covered* my sofa.

remark/re-mark – She *remarked* that she needs to *re-mark*
> the test papers.

reform/re-form – The band is *re-forming* after breaking up
> ten years earlier and *reforming* its ways.

repress/re-press – I need to *re-press* my shirt.
> I need to *repress* my memories.

If you add a prefix to a word and it means there will be two vowels together with the same letter, we can split them with a hyphen: *re-enter, re-entry, re-election, co-own, anti-intellectual, pre-empt, pre-existing, co-op...* (otherwise, they can look confusing; reenter, coown, reelection, coop...). But see the exceptions with 'co + o' below.

If there are two vowels together that can cause confusion, stick in a hyphen: *re-align (realign), de-ice (deice), co-author...*

But we have: *The stamps have been reissued.* A hyphen after *re-* is not needed because there's no confusion with another word.

With the prefix co-
co-op, co-opt, co-organizer, co-owner, co-chairman, co-host, co-pilot, co-star, co-worker, but not coexist.

In British English, we have co-operate, co-operation, co-ordinate or cooperate and coordinate without the hyphen.

In American, no hyphen: cooperate, cooperation, cooperative, coordinate.

With self: self-analysis, self-conscious, self-esteem, self-report (except selfsame, selfhood).

But when adding un to self-conscious, we write unselfconscious (not unself-conscious).

---

for and **fore**

Which is correct?
1. forhead or forehead?
2. forward or foreward?
3. forname or forename?
4. forcast or forecast?
5. forbid or forebid?
6. forfeit or forefeit?

Check the next section for the answers

for/fore – homophones

According to the Oxford Dictionary, **for-** is usually added to words to convey the meaning of "banning", "neglecting", "doing without" or "giving up".

forbid –  refuse to allow

forfeit - give something up
forgive – stop being angry/resentful towards someone
forget – fail to remember

Also, *forgiveness, forbear, forever, forlorn, forbearance, forget, forgot, forgotten, forgetful, forsake, forswear, forum, forgo, forward, fortunate, unfortunately…*

fore- is more common and used when the meaning is "be**fore**", "in advance", or "in front of". *fore* = in front/first/be**fore**

forecourt – open area in front of building
forecast – what will or might happen in the future
forehead – in front of your head
before – in front of/earlier
forename – your first name that comes in front of your surname
foresight, foreman, forearm, foreboding, forethought, foresee, foreseeable, unforeseen, unforeseeable, foreshore, foreword, foreshadow, forerunner, foreground, forewarn, forefather, forefinger, therefore…

Suffixes

-s -y -ing -ment -ful -ly -ed -tion -ble...

prefix + **root word** + suffix
un**comfort**able
ir**regular**ly
mis**understand**ing
dis**respect**fully

misre**present**ations (notice the 2 prefixes
and 2 suffixes)

Suffixes, or common endings, are little words we put at the end of words to change the meaning and grammar.

Noticing suffix endings is so important because when English is spoken quickly, the ending sometimes sounds unstressed or disappears, or has the same sound as other suffixes.

Suffixes are extremely useful.

We can change the grammar:
walk - walks, walked, walking, walker
small - smaller, smallest, smallish
forgive – forgiving, forgiven, forgivable, forgiveness
smile – smiley, smiler, smiling, smiled, smilingly

We can make verbs:
simple - to simplify, simplified
sharp - to sharpen
real – to realize/realise
fright – to frighten

We can make job descriptions:
teach – teacher, electric - electrician, assist - assistant
act - actor, actress, waiter/waitress

We can make adjectives:
beauty - *beautiful*, fame - *famous*, self – *selfish*

A lot of –**ing** and –**ed** words are adjectives too: *frightening, scared, exhilarated, exhilarating*...

We can have more than one suffix ending:
hopefully = hope + ful + ly,
presentationally = present + ation + al +ly

and more than one prefix and suffix together:
misrepresentations = mis + re + present + ation + s

If we take the root word, **employ**, and add other suffixes, we can make other words, such as **employed, employee, employer**, employment, employability...

We can add the **un** prefix to make the opposite meaning, **un**employed, unemployment.

Both the spelling and the meanings of these words are linked. Remember, linked words like these are called a **word family**. We saw more in the section on Word Families.

Remember, we just add prefixes to the root word without changing anything, but with suffixes, we sometimes have to change the end letter, drop it, or double it. We'll see some of these in this section, and more in the Spelling Rules section.

For these rules, we need to know vowel and consonant suffixes.

Some vowel suffixes are: **-ing, -ed, -er, -est, -ise/-ize, -or, ary/ery, -ur, -ent/-ence, ant/ance, -ous, -age, -ive, -ation**...

Some consonant suffixes are: **-s, ly, -ness, -est, -ment, ful, -cian, -tion, -sion, -less, -ful, -ward**...

With consonant suffixes, we usually just add them to the root word unless they end in 'y', then we change them to 'i': dark – *darkness*, happy – *happiness*, hope – *hopeless*, penny – *penniless*

-ment

develop + ment = *development*
commit + ment = *commitment*
govern + ment = *government*
excite - *excitement*
achieve - *achievement*
endorse – *endorsement*

movement, harassment, embarrassment, equipment, improvement, assessment, acknowledgement,
merry – merriment (y to i)

Judgement usually keeps the 'e', but *judgment* is used by lawyers and in AmE.

According to the Oxford Dictionary: In British English, the normal spelling in general contexts is **judgement**. However, the spelling **judgment** is conventional in legal contexts, and in North American English.

-ness

Notice the double 'n' in mean + ness = *meanness,* drunken + ness = *drunkenness, suddenness, keenness, stubbornness, greenness, leanness, thinness*

awareness, coolness, tenderness, softness, madness, levelness, darkness, kindness, goodness, illness, weakness, grossness, stillness, wellness, stiffness, dullness, weakness, firmness...

helpfulness, blissfulness, (two suffixes)

Change y to i

happy + ness = *happiness*
dizziness, laziness, ugliness, liveliness, clumsiness, loneliness, emptiness, cosiness/coziness (AmE), *tidiness, artiness...*

-less

soulless, harmless, fearless, homeless, restless, ageless, faultless

y to i: *penniless, pitiless, merciless*

Combine **less + ness**

harmlessness, fearlessness, homelessness, restlessness, agelessness, mindlessness, faultlessness

Some Suffix Spelling Rules

Only use full when full

Which is the correct spelling for these words?
hopeful or hopefull?
useful or usefull?
beautiful or beautifull?

The suffix **–ful** is always spelt with one 'l'.

Answers
hopeful = hope + ful
useful = use + ful
beautiful = beauty, so change the 'y' to 'i' when adding a consonant suffix beauti + ful

By adding **–ful** to words, we can make adjectives:
wonderful, useful, successful, unsuccessful, dreadful, careful, helpful, unhelpful, hopeful, delightful, forgetful, frightful, thoughtful, peaceful, stressful, grateful...

But when we add the suffix **–ly** to make adverbs or some adjectives, we then get **-fully (double 'l')**
hope + ful + ly = *hopefully*, care + ful + ly = *carefully, usefully, successfully, beautifully, frightfully...*

We usually keep the root word when adding –ful, but there are some British exceptions:
skilful – skillful (AmE)
wilful – willful (AmE)

Only use full when full
Full up. Full marks. A full sandwich.
The train is full.

170

Changing 'y' to 'i' rule

Happiness is a **beautiful** thing, but **loneliness** isn't.

If a word ends in a **consonant** + **y**, then 'y' changes to 'i' when adding suffixes (but not with 'i' suffixes -ing, -ish/ible because we can't have 2 i's together).

Notice these words have two or more syllables (more on syllables in the next chapter).

beauty – beauti + ful = *beautiful, beautician*
happy – *happiness, happily, happier, happiest*
angry – *angrier, angriest, angrily*
ugly – *uglier, ugliest, ugliness*
busy – *busier, busiest, busily, business*
easy – *easier, easiest, easily*
crazy – *crazies, crazily, craziness, crazier, craziest*
lazy – *lazily, laziness, lazier, laziest*
lonely – *lonelier, loneliest, loneliness*
pretty – *prettier, prettiest, prettily*
necessary – *necessarily, unnecessarily*
reply – *replies, replied,* (NOT with –ing *replying* √ *repliing* X)
marry – *married, marriage,* (but not with –ing *marrying*)
apply – *applies, application, applied* (but *applying*)
empty – *emptied, empties, emptier, emptiest, emptiness,* (but not *emptying*)

Don't change for one syllable words: shy – *shyly,* sly – *slyly,* coy – *coyly,* wry – *wryly* (silent 'w')

Exceptions: day ➔ *daily*
              gay ➔ *gaily*

Adding -es to words
For third person (he, she, it) verbs and plurals.

He watches lots of football matches while she watches quizzes and relaxes with boxes of chocolates.

Look at the words below.
What letter or letters are beside the -es?
*bus - buses, business - businesses, box - boxes,
fizz - fizzes,
match - matches, wash – washes*

We add **-es** to words ending in s, ss, sh, ch, x, z.

We put **-es** on the end of these words because it separates the 's' from the other s's and z's (~~gass, passs, quizzs~~ X)

gas - *gases, bus - buses*
pass - *passes, glass – glasses, confess- confesses*
dish - *dishes, wash - washes, wish - wishes*
match - *matches, watch - watches, catch - catches*
box - *boxes, fox- foxes, relax - relaxes*
quiz – *quizzes, whiz - whizzes, fizz – fizzes*
(Check out the 1:1:1 doubling up rule, in the Spelling Rules section, on why we double up the 'z' in *quiz* and *whiz*)

Exception: if the -ch ending is pronounced with a "k" sound, you add **-s**: stomach – *stomachs*, epoch – *epochs*.

This is an easy rule - we add -es to present tense third person verbs and plural endings with words ending in **s, ss, sh, ch, x, z.**

Suffixes that change grammar

Notice that one suffix can have a few functions.

Suffix	Grammar	Original word	Word with suffix
-s	regular plural-	tablet	tablets
	third person verb-	run	runs
-en	irregular plurals-	child	children
	also makes verbs-	fright	frighten
	makes irregular past-	fall	fallen
	makes adjectives-	gold	golden
	feminine nouns-	fox	vixen
-ed	regular past tense-	walk	walk**ed**
	makes adjectives-	talent	talented
-ing	continuous/ progressive tense-	study	study**ing**
	makes adjectives-	frighten	frightening
-er	comparative adjectives-	small	small**er**
	makes jobs-	teach	teacher
-est	superlative adjectives-	small	small**est**
-al	adjectives-	tide	tidal
	nouns-	arrive	arrival
-age	nouns-	spill	spillage
-y	adjectives-	milk	milky
-ly	adverbs-	slow	slow**ly**
	sometimes adjectives-	brother	brotherly

Suffixes to Make Verbs

Some suffixes change a word to a verb (but the new meaning is related to the old meaning).

Suffix	original word	making verbs
-ise or -ize	modern idol	to modernise / modernize idolise / idolize
-en	wide fright deep	to widen frighten deepen
-ate	participant	to participate
-ify	simple	to simplify

Suffixes for jobs

suffix	verb or noun	job or description
-er	teach work	teacher worker
-or	act govern	actor governor
-ist	art	artist
-cian	electric beauty	electrician beautician
-ee	employ absent	employee absentee
-ant	assist	assistant
-ess	act	actress

Suffixes to make adjectives

suffix	verb or noun	adjective
-al	accident	accidental
-ary	imagine	imaginary
-able	tax	taxable
	like	likeable/likable
-ly	love	lovely
	friend	friendly
-y	ease	easy
ful	beauty	beautiful
-ish	self	selfish
	child	childish
-less	use	useless
	taste	tasteless
-ous	fame	famous
-ic	angel	angelic

Suffixes to make nouns

suffix	verb or adjective	noun
-ation	imagine	imagination
-ment	develop	development
-ness	happy	happiness
-age	bag	baggage
-ure	fail	failure

Suffixes Affecting Pronunciation

Adding a suffix to some root words can change the pronunciation of the vowel sound, or make a silent letter voiced, for example:

crumb – crumble, sign – signature, compete - competition

> "Words that are related in meaning are often related in spelling as well, despite changes in sound." Chomsky
>
> This in turn supports a powerful spelling strategy, according to the authors of *Words Their Way*. If you are unsure how to spell a word, try to think of a word that is similar in meaning and structure to one that you *do* know how to spell.

Pronunciation vs. spelling
differ – **differ**ent (silent 'e' we say "diff rent")
(AmE) favor – **favor**ite (silent 'o' we usually say "fav rite")
(BrE) favour – **favour**ite (silent 'ou' we usually say "fav rite")

Long to *short* vowel sound (drop the 'e' and add a suffix)
(Remember the vowel closest to the end 'e' - the magic 'e'/silent 'e' -is usually long, but the long 'e' isn't retained in these words.)

Long - Short

compete – *competition*
define – *definition*
ignite – *ignition*
invite – *invitation*
adore - *adoration*
reside – *resident*
sane – *sanity*
divine – *divinity*
serene – *serenity*
obscene – *obscenity*
extreme - *extremity*
grave – *gravity*

long vowel/hard 'c' – short vowel/soft 'c'
introduce – *introduction*
produce – *production*
reduce – *reduction*

Sometimes a letter can be silent in one word but not in others. These letters help to connect different forms of the same word. This is probably because it makes the pronunciation easier.

silent - *voiced*
sign – *signal, signature*
resign - *resignation*
condem**n** - *condemnation*
crumb – *crumble, crumbling*
bomb – *bombard*
muscle – *muscular*
solemn – *solemnity*
debt - *debit*
limb - *limber*

To sum up this section on prefixes and suffixes, a few words from Darren Johnson, "a student of spelling". Read his story in *the Your Stories* section.

So you start to see you only need to add a few letters and you have a new word, and you start to learn that you don't need to learn an 8 or 9 letter word, you just need to add a few letters to the 4 or 6 letter word you have learnt.

Exercise

Take away the suffix to find the root word.
Don't forget your spelling rules, or if a letter was
dropped, or doubled up, or changed!

biggest _____

friendship _____

quietly _____

sadness _____

hoping _____

secondary _____

employment _____

funnily _____

confusing _____

magician _____

beginner _____

professional _____

imaginary _____

happiness _____

beautiful _____

simplify _____

quizzes _____

decision _____

(Thanks to bbc.co.uk/skillswise)

Exercise answers

biggest - big

friendship - friend

quietly - quiet

sadness - sad

hoping - hope

secondary - second

employment - employ

funnily - funny

confusing - confuse

magician - magic

beginner - begin

professional - profession

imaginary - imagine

happiness - happy

beautiful - beauty

simplify - simple

quizzes - quiz

decision - decide

We'll look at the 1:1:1 doubling up rule and the magic 'e' silent 'e' in the Key Spelling Rules section.

Exercise

Break these words into their prefix, suffix and root word.

	prefix	root word	suffix
e.g. international	inter	nation	al
unthinkable			
misunderstanding			
illegally			
disappointed			
transformed			
unbelievable			
impatiently			
unwillingness			
unfriendly			
multinational			
resignation			
irresistible			

Exercise Answers

Break these words into their prefix, suffix and root word.

	prefix	root word	suffix
international	inter	nation	al
unthinkable	un	think	able
misunderstanding	mis	understand	ing
illegally	il	legal	ly
disappointed	dis	appoint	ed
transformed	trans	form	ed
unbelievable	un	believe	able
impatiently	im	patient	ly
unwillingness	un	willing	ness
unfriendly	un	friend	ly
multinational	multi	nation	al
resignation	re	sign	ation
irresistible	ir	resist	ible

Syllable Breakdown

Syllable breakdown is a good strategy for spelling long words, and helps you remember the prefixes and suffixes, and silent letters.

Breaking a word down into syllables means
- you break a word down into little spoken chunks,
- each chunk is called a syllable,
- each chunk usually has a vowel in it.

1 syllable: *trick*

2 syllables: *paper* – pa/per

3 syllables: *relevant* – re/le/vant

4 syllables: *difficulty* – dif/fi/cul/ty

5 syllables: *educational* – ed/u/ca/tion/al

You can break words down however you want to – there is no right or wrong way. Break the word down the way that helps you.

When you break a long word into syllables, you can tackle one small part at a time, and if you make a mistake, you can easily see which part of the word you need to work on.
Basic Skills Agency

If you find it hard to identify syllables or hear them, no problem, see the words within words, see the vowels, the root words, prefixes and suffixes.

Anne Betteridge says: "If breaking words into syllables doesn't make sense to you, then don't worry. Some people find it hard. A word can be broken up in several ways."
hearing
- small words - h **ear** ing
- suffix endings - hear**ing**
- letter patterns - **hear, near, dear, fear**
- say it oddly - "he" "a" "ring"
- memory trick - you **hear** with your **ear** - hearing

Syllable breakdown:
mis/un/der/stand/ing, dis/con/nec/tion, ex/am/in/a/tion
vs.
Word breakdown:
mis/under/stand/ing, dis/connect/ion, exam/in/ation

Breaking words into syllables also helps you remember the silent letter(s) in the word. Let's look at Wednesday.

Wed<u>nes</u>day works well with syllable breakdown and using it makes sure you remember the silent 'd' and 'e'.
We say "wens day", so when we break it down into **syllables** we have to say it slowly and exaggeratedly, incorporating all the letters: "Wed" "nes" "day"

January and *February* can be broken down too, and will help you with the –uary pattern.
Say these slowly and exaggeratedly
Jan/u/a/ry
Feb/ru/a/ry

Learn the letter pattern –<u>uary</u> "u/a/ry" for *Feb<u>ruary</u>* and *Jan<u>uary</u>*

and also *<u>brr</u>, it's Feb<u>ru</u>ary!*

I use syllable breakdown for 2 words I have trouble with; *reluctant* and *hesitant.* I keep wanting to put an extra 'n' in *reluctant* and an extra 's' in hesitant!
re/luc/tant   hes/i/tant

Syllable breakdown helps with prefixes and suffixes:
hope/ful/ly   de/part/ment   un/friend/ly   un/help/ful
dis/a/point/ed   mis/un/der/stand/ing   un/ will/ing/ness

Common compound words

Break compound words down too. This helps you see if there are any double letters or silent letters: *earring "ear ring", withhold "with hold", cupboard "cup board", hitchhiker "hitch hiker", bookkeeper, overrate, cupboard, handbag, breakfast, newspaper*

somebody	*anybody*	*everybody*
someone	*anyone*	*everyone*
someday	*(any day)*	*everyday**
somehow	*anyhow*	*---*
somewhere	*anywhere*	*everywhere*
something	*anything*	*everything*
sometimes	*anytime (every time)*	

*everyday means "common" or "normal" and is an adjective and describes a noun so is usually before the noun.
everyday chores
everyday working week
everyday materials

every day (two words) means "each day" and is an adverb which means it describes the verb.
I do the chores every day.
Every day, I go to work, or, I go to work every day.
I use these materials every day.

Which is correct?
1. a. *Technology is advancing everyday.*
   b. *Technology is advancing every day.*

2. a. *Everyday, when people come home, the first thing they do is turn on the TV.*
   b. *Every day, when people come home, the first thing they do is turn on the TV.*

3. a. *Computers are a part of everyday life.*
   b. *Computers are a part of every day life.*

Which is correct?

1. a. *Technology is advancing ~~everyday~~.* X
   b. *Technology is advancing* **every day**. ✓
   The trick is to replace **every day** with **each day**.
   Technology is advancing (each day) every day. ✓
   Not *Technology is advancing (normal/common) ~~everyday~~.* X

2. a. *~~Everyday~~, when people come home, the first thing they do is turn on the TV.* X
   b. ***Every day**, when people come home, the first thing they do is turn on the TV.* ✓ *Each day, when people come home...* ✓

3. a. *Computers are a part of **everyday** life.* ✓
   Computers are part of (normal) everyday life. ✓
   b. *Computers are a part of ~~every day~~ (each day) life.* X

Notes

Phonic Spelling Strategies

Patterns, rhymes, sounds and rules

Even though English is only about 50% phonetically regular, good spellers always try to sound out a word if they're not sure of the spelling because sound is the first bit of a word we have reference for, and certain patterns go with certain sounds. So they try to hear if it sounds like a word or pattern they know how to spell, and then when they write it, they use their visual memory and knowledge of rules and patterns to see if it's right.

So listening to sounds can help you spell but it's an unreliable strategy which needs backing up with other strategies.

An understanding of phonics can help with the spelling of **regular** words. You might not have come across a word before but, if it is regular, then you stand a good chance of being able to work it out. For instance, you might never have seen the word "chitterling", but you can read it (and possibly even be able to spell it) because you will recognize bits of the word: **ch** as in **church   itter** as in **litter   ling** as in **falling**
Anne Betteridge: *Adult Learners' Guide to Spelling*

We have 26 letters of the alphabet and over 44 different sounds (and more with our many English accents). So some letters have to do more than one job, and we also have to combine letters.

We have single consonants, and consonant blends:
beginning: br-, bl-, sc-, st-, sw-, gl-, pr-, spr-, str-, thr-, shr-
end: -st, -sp, -sk, -pt, -lf, -lp, -nk, -ng, -nt, -ck, -tch, -dge

We can use rhyming to help:
flag, brag, drag, shag, snag, blag, stag
-ink, pink, sink, wink, drink, stink, think
-ing, ping, sing, wing, ring, sting, thing

There are 20 vowel sounds (and many more because of accents). But we only have 5 vowel letters (a. e. i. o. u.) and sometimes 'y' is classed as a vowel depending on its position within a word. So we combine vowels -ee- -ea- -ie- -ei- -uo- -ui- -oi- -ow- -oy-

But these vowel patterns can have different sounds. They can be long, short or a diphthong (2 vowel sounds in one syllable – *coin, side, loud*). So developing your visual memory, knowledge of rules, and patterns is important.

Every word, and every syllable within a word, must have a vowel sound, otherwise, we would not be able to say or hear words clearly at all. Lyn Stone: *Spelling for Life*

Building your spelling knowledge of letter patterns and their sounds, understanding long and short vowel sounds and how they can be influenced by single and double consonants, and seeing spelling rule patterns, can all help with your spelling.

What are long and short vowel sounds?
Let's look at these without going too "linguistic" and academic! Don't worry if you don't know these, or can't hear them. I wasn't taught them at school. I bet you weren't either, which is a shame because they can influence and help spelling and reading.

Long vowel sounds: *dream, need, soon, please, rain*. They can also have a single vowel: *phone, kind, say*. They say their alphabet name "a, e, i, o, u" = "ay", "ee", "eye", "oh" "you". We also combine these to make diphthongs: -oi- -oy- -ow- -ai-

Notice how the spelling of the sounds can vary:
e - "ee" *please, dream, key/quay, these, thief, evening, equal*
i - "eye" *kind, buy/bye, pint, dive, light, high, guide*
o - "oh" *phone, bold, toe/tow, ozone, broke, flown, old*
a - "ay" *say, tail/tale, break, page, alien, racing, eight*
u – "you" "who" *use, cute, super, tuna, fruit, new*
"eye" for 'y' in *cry, why, shy, supply, try*

Be careful of these homophones. They have the same sound but different meaning and spelling of the long vowel sound: *steak/stake, break/brake, aisle/I'll/isle, ate/eight, be/bee, bean/been, blew/blue, brews/bruise, buy/by/bye, ceiling/sealing, cereal/serial, chews/choose, cue/queue...*

Consonants can also make a vowel long, for example,
-**gh**- makes the 'i' long in *sigh, sight, high, light, flight*
-**nd** makes the 'i' long in *wind* (a clock), *kind, mind, find, grind*
-**w** *saw, law, flaw, new, chew, blew, stew, few, blow, grown, know, snow, low, grow...*
r-influenced: *car, star, dark, scare, near, year, herb, herd, third, shirt, bird, skirt, girl, curd*
l-influenced: *walk, talk, folk, yolk, fold, told, sold, cold, roll*

Short vowels: a in <u>a</u>pple, **e** in <u>e</u>gg, i <u>i</u>n <u>i</u>nch, **o** in <u>o</u>dd, **u** in <u>u</u>nder

According to Shireen Shuster: Short vowel sounds are usually simple to spell. But there are a few traps.	
red but *dead*	*bed* but *head*
mist but *mystery*	*Jim* but *gym*
on but *swan*	*rod* but *squad*
nutty but *nothing*	*bubble* but *trouble*

We're going to look at some interesting consonant patterns and how we use them with short and long vowel sounds.

Long and short vowel sound comparison

short	ban	Ben	bin	bonny	bun
long	bane	bean/ been	bind	boney	
short	bat	bet	bit	bot	but
long	bait	beat/ beet	bite	bowtie	beauty
short	pat	pet	pit	pot	put
long	pate	Pete/ peat	pint	poetry	putrid
short	pack	peck	pick	pock	puck
long	park	peak/ peek	pike	poke	puke
short	gnat	net	knit	not/ knot	nut
long	nature	neat	night	note	newt
short	can	Ken	kin	con	come
long	cane	keen	kind	cone	coma
short	had	head	hid	hod	hud/hood
long	shade	heed	hide	hole	who

Look at and say these. What do you notice, any rules?

short – long
hop – hope
till - tile
Mick – Mike
supper – super
goggle – Google
pitch – peach
cadge – cage

We're going to look at these patterns and rules next.

Some spelling rules

Read the words below and hear the difference.

short vowel sounds / long vowel sounds

hop / *hope*

cut / *cute*

slim / *slime*

not / *note*

When we put a silent 'e' at the end of words, we make a new word with a long vowel sound. This silent 'e' at the end of words, following a single vowel and a consonant, usually makes the vowel long (but we have some exceptions with common function words: *come, have, some, done, love, glove*).

When we drop the 'e' with -ing or vowel suffixes the long vowel sound is kept:

hope – hoping

tape – taping

use – usage

make – making

manage – manager

write – writable

believe – believable

note – notable

hate – hatred

But the 'e' doesn't affect the long sound in "se" words. The 'e' was added so we don't get confused with the plural of some words.

ten/tens - tense	*lap/laps - lapse*
brow/brows – browse	*cop/cops – copse*

Y makes a long "eye" vowel sound in: *dry, cry, my, crying, dryer*

The silent 'e' doesn't have to come at the end of a word – *Peter, baker, driver, winery, hopefully, used...*

Some common exceptions: *ever, never, clever, seven, eleven*

Short Vowel Sounds
One little letter can alter the meaning and sound of words.

sit	set	sat	slot	shut
pit	pet	pat	pot	put
mitt	met	mat	mot	mutt
hill	hell	Hal	hold	hull/Hull
pick	peck	pack	pock	puck
kin	Ken	can	con	come
bid	bed	bad	bod	bud
Sid	said	sad	sod	sudden
hid	head	had	hod	hud/hood
bitch	etch	batch	botch	butch
bib	--	babble	bobble	bubble
bitter	better	batter	blotter	butter
bigger	beggar	bagger	blogger	bugger

Flossy words
One syllable words ending in **F, L** or **S** (FLOSSY) double these letters after a short vowel:
pull, hull, full, dull, bull, bill, hill, pill, will, kill, till, ill, still, fill, bell, hell, sell, cell, well, tell, fell, yell, smell, shell, spell... shall, drill
(Exceptions: long sound in *all, ball, call, tall, fall, wall, small, stall*)

off, staff, Jeff, cuff, gruff, buff, fluff, huff, muff, puff, stuff, scruff, cliff, toff, naff
kiss, hiss, piss, miss, bliss, Swiss, cross, toss, loss, floss, fuss, mess, less, guess, dress, lass, mass,
painless, harmless, homeless, darkness, illness, kindness
express, impress, process, depress, success, discuss
pass, glass, grass (in some accents, these are a long "ar" sound "glarss")

Exceptions: *of, if, us, pal, gas, bus, yes, chef, clef, plus*

Double consonants

Usually, one vowel followed by two consonants in words of more than one syllable indicates it's a short vowel sound:
dad - daddy, gran – granny, mum – mummy, rabbit, sorry, silly, letter, supper, dinner, poppy, difficult, chubby, rubbish, follow...
But there are lots of exceptions: *melon, salad, cabin, treble, habit, body...*

Spelling rule

hop – hopping; sit - sitting, sitter;
swim - swimming, swimmer
stop - stopping, stopped, stopper, stoppable; slop - sloppy
big - bigger, biggest, biggish; bet – better, betting

This is the 1:1:1 doubling up rule = 1 syllable: 1 vowel: next to 1 end consonant (see Spelling Rules section for more on this rule).

Exceptions: We never double up the 'k' in English words, but use **-ck** to indicate a short vowel sound: *check, chick, chock, chuck, chicken, wreck, Rick, rack, rock, ruck, racket...*

We never double up the letter X or **V** except in *revving, revved, navvy.*

Look at these, read them and notice the short vowel sound has two consonants.

long / short
super / supper
diner / dinner
coma / comma
later / latter
striped / stripped
slimiest / slimmest
hoping / hopping
taping / tapping
biter / bitter
lose / loss

Remember, double consonants usually mark a short vowel sound.

Knowing this not only helps your spelling but your reading too.

I was **hopping** mad and was **hoping** he wasn't home.

Let's go to the **diner** and have **dinner**.

That's a **super** idea for **supper**.

What do you notice about these words?
Read them aloud.

itch - each
pitch – peach
bitch – beach
tetchy - teach

-tch vs. **-ch**

> *itch - each*
> *pitch – peach*
> *bitch – beach*

The **-tch** ending indicates a short vowel sound, and follows a one-letter vowel.

-atch	-etch	-itch	-utch	-otch
snatch	stretch	stitch	-	Scotch
catch	ketchup	kitchen	clutch	crotch
batch	etch	bitch	butch	botch
patch dispatch	wretch sketch	witch twitch	crutch	blotch watch* (*pronounced "wotch")

We have some exceptions with common words ending in -ch: *rich, enrich, such, much, which, touch, attach, sandwich, ostrich, spinach, duchess, detach, bachelor, attach, detach.*

-ch is exactly the same sound as **-tch**. The 't' doesn't affect the sound of "ch". Read them aloud and see – *which/witch, itch/each, butch/such, pitch/peach...*

Homophone: *which – witch*
Which witch is which?

> The Oxford Dictionary says these words often cause problems. A common mistake is to spell *attach* and *detach* with *–tch*.
>
> If the final *"ch"* comes after a consonant, the ending is *–ch*: *inch, search, church, branch, pinch, winch.*
>
> If the final *"ch"* comes after a two-letter vowel, the ending is *–ch*: *each, beach/beech, teach, reach, speech, touch, crouch.*

Spelling rule

We add –es to –ch to make plurals and third person 's' (he, she, it).

watch – watches	match – matches	blotch - blotches
peach – peaches	rich – riches	witch - witches
snatch – snatches	catch – catches	sketch - sketches

Compare these short vowel sounds to long ones. Careful with the spelling with some of these! There are probably more problems with speaking these, though! *To reach the beach. To rich the bitch. The pitch is on the bitch. The pitch is on the beach…*
rich – reach
bitch – beach
pitch – peach

Use rhyming to help spell when you know one of these spellings.
match, snatch, catch, batch…
Careful, watch is pronounced "wotch".
Dutch, hutch, butch, but also *such, much, touch*
fetch, stretch, etch, sketch
rich, bitch, stitch, witch, itch

Long vowel sounds
each, peach, beach/beech, reach, teach, speech

Write –tch and –ch letter pattern
stories or sentences.

195

-dge vs. –ge

English words don't end in **j**, we use **–dge** or **–ge**.

Notice **judge** has a "j" sound at the beginning and end.

-dge = short vowel sound:
badge, Madge, cadge, badger
edge, hedge, ledge, wedge, pledge, ledger, sledge
Exceptions: Abbreviations: *veg, reg*
ridge, bridge, fridge, porridge, midge
dodge, lodge, lodger, podgy
judge, budge, fudge, nudge, grudge, smudge, sludge, misjudge

No 'd' if there's another consonant.
plunge, bulge, gunge, orange, sponge, hinge, dungeon

When the root word is more than one syllable then we use –**age** or **–ege** not –dge: *village, garage, cottage, collage, garbage, damage, bandage, marriage, college, allege...*

Long vowel sounds

–ge = a long sound in: ***age***, *page, sage, stage, cage, huge, rage, cage, wage, refuge, rampage...*

-ange
Long "a" sound with **–nge** : *range, change, grange, strange, danger, angel...*

-rge
r-influenced long sound with **–rge**: *charge, large, Marge, barge, forge, surge, merge, gorgeous, George, splurge...*

-ck, -ke, -k

> Why do we have *-k, -ke, -ck* when they sound the same?
>
> **Jack** and **Jake** make **pancakes** and **bake cakes** all **week**, and then **like** playing **hockey** and **whacking** a ball at **weekends**.

Long vs. Short Vowel Sounds

short / long
Mick – Mike
Jack – Jake
luck – Luke
lick – like
back – bake
cock – coke
whack – wake
sack – sake
shack – shake
black – Blake
block – bloke
quack – quake*

Notice the words in both columns have **one vowel** before the -ck and -ke. But the -**ke** ending has a long vowel sound because of the magic 'e' silent 'e' at the end: *cake, take, bake, coke, provoke, bloke, spoke, mistake, pancake, awake, like, bike, pike, hitchhike...*

We drop the 'e' with -ing and still maintain the long sound: *liking, baking, making, provoking...*

Remember, we don't double up the **k** to indicate a **short vowel** sound but use the -**ck** ending:
Mick, lick, pick, knick, flick, kick, chick, gimmick, carsick
whack, sack, back, tack, jack, knack, flack, black, attack, ransack
luck, duck, suck, tuck, truck, potluck
dock, lock, rock, sock, clock, block, hammock, padlock
neck, peck, deck, speck, fleck

-**ck**- can be found in the middle of words: *jacket, whacking, pocket, blockage, crackers, pucker, docket, socket, chicken...*

Normally, there's just one vowel before the –ck, but in *quick* and *quack* you can see two vowels together. In English words, Q always comes with U, so it's classed as one consonant -qu-.
quack, quick, quacking, quickly = short vowel sounds

Double k happens in some foreign borrowed words:
trek – trekking, trekked

Mick vs. *Mike*
Mick = a short sound because of –ck
Mike = a long sound because of the magic 'e' silent 'e'

-**k**
 two vowels + **k** = a long sound
leak, peak/peek, beak, teak
cheek, seek, meek, cheek, reek, week/weak
break, steak, soak, sleek, croak, geek, streak

Exceptions: *book, cook, look, nook, hook, took, rook, shook, brook...* These used to be pronounced with a long "oo" sound, and in some accents, they still are.

'r' influenced long sound: *dark, bark, park, snarky, lark, mark, shark perk, Dirk, Turk, lurk,*

'l' influenced long sound: "ork" – walk, talk, chalk, stalk
"oak" - folk, yolk

-nk = short sound:
ink, think, blink, wink
thank, Hank, bank
sunk, dunk, funk, chunk, skunk, slunk, trunk, junk, bunk

Some long vowel sound patterns

tale/tail	teem/team	tile	toe/tow	true
day	dean	dine	doe	do
cake	key/quay	kind	co	coupon
bait/bate	beat/beet	buy/bye	bold	beauty
page	please	pint	phone	blue

Patterns with -ol- usually indicate a long vowel sound. -O- says its alphabet name "oh", which is a long vowel sound.
old, bold, cold, fold, old, hold, mold, sold, told, wold, scold, soldier,
bolt, colt, dolt, holt, jolt, volt
folk, yolk
boll, droll, poll, scroll, toll

-oast
boast, coast toast, roast

-ost
host, ghost, post, most

-aste
taste, waste, baste, paste, chaste, chasten

-ange
change, danger, range, strange, exchange, arrange, grange, angel

-ind
find, bind, kind, rind, mind, behind, blind

-igh
high, sigh, light, night, fight, fright, sight, right, bright, blight, flight, plight, tight, knight, might, uptight, tonight, alright...

-ite
bite, site, write, white, polite, quite, unite, excite, kite...

Long to short vowel sound change

Some root words change their vowel sound when we add suffixes, or change the word to a verb, noun, adjective, etc.

Notice how the vowel sound changes, and how hard it would be to say the words in the second column if there wasn't a sound change! This happened during the Great Vowel Shift from 1300, when vowel sounds changed but the spelling was already fixed.

long - short
five – fifth/fifty/fifteen
south – southern
type – typical
hero – heroine
heal – health/healthy
decide – decision
grateful – gratitude
shade – shadow
clean – cleanliness
female – feminine
define – definite, definitive
divine – divinity
mime – mimic
holy – holiday
crime – criminal
please – pleasant, pleasure
mean – meant

Drop the i

Look at these words and notice how we drop the 'i' in the -ai-pattern when adding certain vowel endings. Notice the sound change.

long - *short*

explain – explanation, explanatory, self-explanatory

Spain – Spaniard, Spanish

exclaim – exclamation

proclaim – proclamation

reclaim – reclamation

acclaim – acclamation

prevail – prevalent, prevalence

-ai- to -e-

We also replace the -ai- with -e- in the following words (notice the long to short sound change):

maintain - maintenance

(Although *maintenance* often implies the *maintaining* of something, the word does not have *maintain* in it)

detain - detention

retain - retention

attain - attention

sustain - sustenance

abstain - abstention

-ei- to -e-

We have long to short in:

receive – reception

deceive - deception

conceive – conception

perceive - perception

Look at *pronounce* and *pronunciation*. Notice the spelling of *pronunciation* – the 'o' is dropped.

Before writing the word out, say both *pronunciation* and *pronounce* out loud, and hear the difference. We can use syllable breakdown for *pronunciation* "pro" **"nun"** "ci" "a" "tion".

See words within words for *pronounce* – an **ounce** of pron**ounce**.

Or use rhyming and sentences: *ounce, announce, bounce, pounce.*

I want to announce how to pronounce an ounce of bounce.

When you announce it, please don't mispronounce an ounce of it.

Notes and sentences

Next, we're going to look at the rules around **-le words**.

Read the following pairs of words aloud. Look at them. What do you notice?

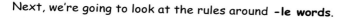

idle / middle
maple / apple
Google / goggle
gable / gabble
noble / nobble

202

-le words

Did you notice the long and short sounds and
the single and double consonants?
long / short
idle / middle
maple / apple
Google / goggle
gable / gabble
noble / nobble

Did you notice the words in the first column have long vowel
sounds and one consonant before –le: *idle, maple, Google,
gable, noble*?

The second column words have short vowel sounds, and so
have double letters: *middle, apple, goggle, gabble, nobble.*

idle and **middle**
idle has a long vowel sound so -**dle**
middle has a short vowel sound so -**ddle**

maple and **apple**
maple has a long vowel sound so –**ple**
apple has a short vowel sound so –**pple**

able, cable, table, fable, gable, sable, stable, enable
babble, dabble, drabble, gabble, grabble, rabble, scrabble

noble, ennoble, Grenoble, ignoble
bobble, cobble, gobble, hobble, nobble, knobble, wobble

bible
nibble, dibble, dribble, kibble, scribble quibble

idle, sidle, bridle
middle, diddle fiddle, piddle, riddle, griddle, twiddle

The spelling/English guru, David Crystal, says something interesting about these short vowel -le words, and how most of them express a sound that reflects real life. They have onomatopoeic qualities (they sound like the sound that they refer to).

Read them aloud and see what he means:
bubble, babble, dabble, crumble, dribble, dazzle, nibble,
rubble, wobble, rabble, chuckle, speckle, twinkle, trickle,
wriggle, squiggle, wiggle, fiddle, twiddle, piddle, diddle,
shuffle, sniffle, snuffle, snuggle, gabble, gobble, giggle,
wobble, topple, rustle, haggle, cuddle, huddle, dapple,
frazzled, sizzle, drizzle, guzzle, grizzle

Of course, like anything about spelling, there are plenty of exceptions.

David Crystal: *Words, Words, Words*

Now write some fun sentences with these words.
(Can you fit in some long sound -le words too?)
Enjoy it.

Exercises

1. Short and long vowel sounds. Change 'a' to 'o' in the following words. Say the old and the new words out loud so you hear and see the new sounds, meanings and patterns.

cat _____   paint _____   broad _____

grain _____   farmer _____   shave _____

ward _____   glass _____   boat _____

care _____   bath _____   fail _____

2. Short sounds. Now change the 'i' to 'e'

pin _____   miss _____   flick _____

pick _____   rid _____   piddle _____

bid _____   fill _____   middle _____

3. Short and long vowel sounds. Now change the 'e' to 'o'

less _____   eat _____   stew _____

ear _____   let _____   sew _____

belt _____   bend _____   pest _____

4. Short and long vowel sounds. Now change the 'o' to 'u'

pot _____   cop _____   long _____

song _____   torn _____   strong _____

role _____   most _____   doll _____

Thanks to the *Spelling Pack*

Exercises Answers

1. Short and long vowel sounds. Change 'a' to 'o' in the following words.

   Say the old and the new words out loud so that you hear and see the new sounds, meanings and patterns.

cat <u>cot</u>	paint <u>point</u>	broad <u>brood</u>
grain <u>groin</u>	farmer <u>former</u>	shave <u>shove</u>
ward <u>word</u>	glass <u>gloss</u>	boat <u>boot</u>
care <u>core</u>	bath <u>both</u>	fail <u>foil</u>

2. Short sounds. Now change the 'i' to 'e'

pin <u>pen</u>	miss <u>mess</u>	flick <u>fleck</u>
pick <u>peck</u>	rid <u>red</u>	piddle <u>peddle</u>
bid <u>bed</u>	fill <u>fell</u>	middle <u>meddle</u>

3. Short and long vowel sounds. Now change the 'e' to 'o'

less <u>loss</u>	eat <u>oat</u>	stew <u>stow</u>
ear <u>oar</u>	let <u>lot</u>	sew <u>sow</u>
belt <u>bolt</u>	bend <u>bond</u>	pest <u>post</u>

4. Short and long vowel sounds. Now change the 'o' to 'u'

pot <u>put</u>	cop <u>cup</u>	long <u>lung</u>
song <u>sung</u>	torn <u>turn</u>	strong <u>strung</u>
role <u>rule</u>	most <u>must</u>	doll <u>dull</u>

Thanks to the *Spelling Pack*

Spelling vs. Pronunciation

We're going to look at the differences between spelling and pronunciation in some common words with silent letters in them. We'll see how we can use spelling strategies to spell them. We'll also revise memory tricks, syllable breakdown, spelling rules, and phonetic strategies.

In set 1, we're going to look at eight words that are pronounced with two syllables but spelled with three. These are simple words that you might be able to spell now, but read on and revise the spelling strategies.

And then in Set 2, we'll look at six longer words that are pronounced with three syllables but spelled with four.

Exercise Which is correct?
Use your spelling strategies to help you.
Or you might see what looks right.

1. a. business   b. bussiness   c. busness

2. a. choclate   b chocolate   c. chocalate

3. a. diffrent   b. different   c. differant

4. a. mariage   b. marriage   c. marrage

5. a. interest   b. interrest   c. intarest

6. a. dictionery   b. dictionry   c. dictionary

7. a. temprature   b. temperature   c. temperuture

8. a. usually   b. usualy   c. useually

Answers

1. a. business   b. bussiness   c. busness

2. a. choclate   b chocolate   c. chocolate

3. a. diffrent   b. different   c. differant

4. a. mariage   b. marriage   c. marrage

5. a. interest   b. interrest   c. intarest

6. a. dictionery   b. dictionry   c. dictionary

7. a. temprature   b. temperature   c. temperuture

8. a. usually   b. usualy   c. useually

If you want to listen to the pronunciation (British & American), check these dictionary websites:
www.macmillandictionary.com
www.dictionary.cambridge.org/dictionary/english/

Set 1

The following eight words are usually pronounced with two syllables but spelled with three.

1. business

We say "biz ness", missing out the 'i' *bus(i)ness*

Can you remember the memory trick from the words within words section?

*It's good **business** to go by **bus.***

*Business isn't a **sin**.*

bus I ness

Busy + ness = *business*. Remember the 'y' to 'i' spelling rule with suffix endings.

Remember to add –es for the plural: *businesses.*

We also have the compound words *businesswoman* and *businessman.*

2. chocolate

We say "choc lat", missing out the 'o' *choc(o)late.*

Use syllable breakdown slowly and exaggeratedly "choc o late".

See the 'o' vowels choco

*I **ate** too much **chocolate**.*

3. different

We say "diff rent", missing out the 'e' *diff(e)rent.*

Use syllable breakdown *dif/fe/rent   diff/e/rent.*

Notice the e's.

*I beg to <u>differ</u> but the **rent** is <u>diff</u>e<u>rent</u> every year.*

4. omelette (BrE)/omelette or omelet (AmE)

We say "om let", missing out the 'e' *om(e)lette/om(e) let*

Notice the e's

Use syllable breakdown:

British: o/me/lette   om/e/lette   om/e/let/te

Let me make an omel<u>ette</u> for <u>tea</u>.

American: o/me/let   ***Let** me make an ome**let**.*

5. every

We say "ev ry", missing out the 'e' ev(e)ry.

e + very = every or *eve + ry = every*

Every evening **Eve** is <u>very</u> tired.

6. marriage

We say "ma rige", missing out the 'a' marri(a)ge.

Spelling rule: *marry + age* change the 'y' to 'i' rule with suffixes.

marry ➜ marri + age = *marriage*

The **age** to marry and have a marri**age**.

7. interest

We say "in trest", missing out the 'e' int(e)rest

Notice the e's.

in/te/rest

inter est

inte rest

*In the interests of international safety, please **rest**.*

8. Wednesday

We say "wens day" missing out the 'd' and 'e' We(d)n(e)sday.

Tip: Break this down into syllables and say them slowly and exaggeratedly *"Wed" "nes" "day".* Notice the e's again.

Set 2
The following six words are usually pronounced with three syllables, but spelled with four.

1. comfortable
We say "comf ta bull", missing out the 'or' *comf(or)table*.
Use syllable breakdown or words within words.
com/for/ta/ble
com/fort/able
comfort/able

2. vegetable
We say "veg tu bull", missing out the 'e' veg(e)table.
But sometimes, people pronounce the 'e' "veg" "uh" "ta "ble".
Use syllable breakdown or words within words:
veg/e/t/able
veg/e/table

3. interesting
We say "in tres ting", missing out the 'e' int(e)resting.
Notice the e's.
in/te/rest/ing
interest/ing

4. dictionary
We say "dic shun ry", missing out the 'a' diction(a)ry.
Use syllable breakdown - dic/tion/a/ry.

Remember, the -ary ending in Latin means belonging to/connected with, so a *dictionary* is connected to a manual or book of words.

The 'a' in –ary can be silent or sounded out in other -ary words. **ary** (Latin for belonging to, connected with)
library (connected with books), *missionary* (belonging to a mission), *stationary* (originally meant belonging to a military station), *primary* (from Latin first), *anniversary* (returning yearly)

5. temperature

We say "tem pre chu", missing out the 'e' temp(e)rature.

tem/per/a/ture, *temp/er/a/ture*

*I get in a **temper** when the **temperature** is high.*

6. usually

We say "you sh ly", missing out the 'a' usu(a)lly.

usual + ly = *usually* (double 'l')

u/su/al/ly

*Notice the u's **u s u** ally*

Even more u's in *unusually* = un + usual + ly.

*It's usually **all** or nothing with **us**.*

Exercise

1. a. dictionaries b. dictionries c. dictioneries

2. a. unusully b. unusually c. unusualy

3. a. Wenesday b. Wednsday c. Wednesday

4. a. mariage b. marriage c. marryage

5. a. indifferent b. indifferant c. indiffrent

6. a. chocolates b. chocalates c. choclates

7. a. uncomfortable b. uncomfortible c. uncomfotable

8. a. vegtables b. vegatables c. vegetables

9. a. interestingly b. intrestingly c. intarestingly

10. a. busness b. bussiness c. business

Exercise Answers

1. *a.* **dictionaries** *b. dictionries* *c. dictioneries*

2. *a. unusully* *b.* **unusually** *c. unusualy*

3. *a. Wenesday* *b. Wednsday* *c.* **Wednesday**

4. *a. mariage* *b.* **marriage** *c. marryage*

5. *a.* **indifferent** *b. indifferant* *c. indiffrent*

6. *a.* **chocolates** *b. chocalates* *c. choclates*

7. *a.* **uncomfortable** *b. uncomfortible* *c. uncomfotable*

8. *a. vegtables* *b. vegatables* *c.* **vegetables**

9. *a. intrestingly* *b.* **interestingly** *c. intarestingly*

10. *a. busness* *b. bussiness* *c.* **business**

Notes

213

Look, Say, Cover, Write, Check method

Using this method is great because it makes you use various senses and activities - seeing the word, hearing it, thinking about it, visualizing it, and writing it.

It really improves your spelling if you use it every day. All you need is a piece of paper and a pen, or notebook.

1. Write the word (even a sentence) on a piece of paper, make sure you spell the word correctly.

2. **Look** at the word carefully - really study it. Any problem letters? Any familiar letter patterns? Any silent letters? Any prefixes, suffixes, root words?

3. **Say** the word out loud a few times. Does it break down into syllables? Any sounds similar to other words you know?

4. **Cover** the word. Say it again and form a visual image of the word.

5. **Write** the word. Don't worry about mistakes.

6. **Check** your spelling with the original. Check it carefully, letter by letter. Underline the mistake and correct it. Think about why you made the mistake and any tricks to help you remember the correct spelling.

7. If incorrect, do these steps again until correct.

8. Repeat these steps after ten minutes, then after a day, a week.

Check out my video for more info in the Lessons section: www.howtospell.co.uk/LSCWvideo.php

Look, Say, Cover, Write, Check

Think about your mistakes – what are they? Why do you think you've made them? Keep doing this method every day. But it's important to make sure you check your spelling letter by letter. Some people rush through, thinking they're right, but have missed a vital letter. This method works if you do it a little bit every day.

Write the word here. Check to see if it's spelled correctly!	achieve			
Write the words downwards so you can check letter by letter	acheive			
Think about the mistakes and do the LSCW again and a few times every day				

Take an Interest in Words

Taking an interest in words is a key spelling strategy to help you stop getting frustrated with English spelling and start loving it, which, of course, will improve your spelling.

Enjoy the quirkiness of English spelling, know why words are spelled the way they are, understand the history of spelling, and you won't get frustrated with spelling, and you'll even learn, remember and understand spellings. Joanne Rudling: *The Reasons Why English Spelling is so Weird and Wonderful*

Exploring the origins of words and the processes of word creation provides a powerful knowledge base for learning spelling and vocabulary, as well as facilitating more effective reading and writing. Bear, Invernizzi, Templeton, Johnston: *Words Their Way.*

Remember from the Silent Letters section, English and spelling developed out of the tribes that invaded and settled in England. Look at the origins of these words below:

The **Romans** from Italy (spoke Latin) - *plumber, scissors, debt, receipt...*

The **Angles, Saxons, Jutes** from Germany and Holland (Dutch/Germanic), *right, daughter, folk, write, walk...*

The **Vikings** from Denmark and Norway (spoke Old Norse) *know, knee, gnat, gnaw...*

And finally, in 1066, the **French** from northern France (spoke Norman French) changed a lot of spellings. Can you remember why we have *queen, quiver, hour, honest, guess, vogue...?*

There's never been a moment when English was pure. English has always been influenced by other languages, and has never been afraid of borrowing words from everywhere.

We've never had an academy of English to control our words, spelling or language, which is why we have a huge variety of words, "strange" spellings, and an enormous dictionary and thesaurus.

Most of the borrowings in Modern English have been in the language for centuries, as a result of the first periods of contact, so we no longer have a sense of their foreign-ness. David Crystal: *Words Words Words*

In the 17th - 19th centuries, the British Empire expanded and introduced words from all parts of the world, and with them some strange spellings:

America – *prairie*
India – *chutney*
Australia – *kangaroo*
New Zealand - *kiwi*
Africa – *safari*
China – *ketchup*

Words and spellings can even show us the trade undertaken and history of exploration. It also gives us a sense of the country:

- India - *guru, bungalow, veranda, juggernaut, pundit, shampoo, chintz, dinghy...*
- Words from Holland and the Dutch include words about art *-easel, etch, landscape.* From seafaring: *smuggle, cruise.*
- Travels to South America borrowed from Spanish and Portuguese include *tobacco, hurricane, banana, alligator, potato.*
- Italian: *violin, solo, sonnet, giraffe, balcony...*

We have food products from all over the world:

- French: *almond, salad, lettuce, basil, spinach, rice, mustard...*
- Spanish: *avocado, potato...* Portuguese: *coconut.* And from both: *yams*
- Italian: *pasta, pesto, broccoli...*
- Tamil: *curry*
- Dutch: *cookie*
- Chinese: *pak choi/bok choi, ketchup...*
- Latin: *wine, cheese, peas...*
- Arabic: *coffee, alcohol, sugar, syrup...*

Can you remember where these words come from?

1. bungalow
2. ketchup
3. galore (not mentioned above, but can you guess?)
4. alcohol
5. guru
6. shampoo

Answers

1. **bungalow** from India, Hindi *baṅglā* "belonging to Bengal", from a type of cottage built for early European settlers in Bengal.

2. **ketchup** from Chinese Cantonese dialect, tomato juice.

3. **galore** from Irish *go leor*, literally "to sufficiency".

4. **alcohol** from Arabic *al-kuḥl* "the kohl". In early use, the term referred to powders, specifically kohl, and especially those obtained by distilling or rectifying spirits.

5. **guru** from India, Hindi and Punjabi, from Sanskrit *guru* "weighty, grave" (compare with Latin *gravis*), hence "elder, teacher".

6. **shampoo** from India, Hindi *cāṃpo!* "press!"

We're going to look at British and American spelling next.

Which are the American spellings and why are there differences?

car tyre or *tire*
colour or *color*
fulfil or *fulfill*
travelling or *traveling*
enrol or *enroll*

American vs. British Spelling

> *color/colour, centre/center, realise/realize*
> Which is the British English spelling and which is the American?
>
> Why are there differences between British and American spellings?

Knowing the differences between American and British English spelling is important because of the internet and computer software. Also, a lot of computers are automatically set to an American dictionary, so if you're working in British English, it will leave you wondering why the spelling has a red squiggly line under it, even though you spelt it correctly!

It's good if you know the differences, as then you can adapt your spelling to whatever person or market you're writing for.

Knowing the differences adds another layer to your spelling knowledge and stops potential confusion.

Exercise Answers

British spellings vs. American spellings

car tyre – tire
colour – color
fulfil – fulfill
travelling – traveling
enrol – enroll

So why are there differences? Do you know?

There are spelling differences because of the American Revolution (1775-1783), when the Americans overthrew British rule and wanted to be different from Britain - and one way was to reform spelling. Noah Webster led the way.

In 1783, he published a book called the *American Spelling Book*, which sold millions, and in 1828, he published his *American English Dictionary*.

Noah Webster

The main spelling reforms were reducing the number of letters and changing some letters around.

British to **American**
-*our* to -*or* (colour to **color**)
-*re* to -*er* (centre to **center**)
-*ise* to -*ize* (realise to **realize)**
-*yse* to -*yze* (analyse to **analyze)**
-*ogue* to -*og* or -*ogue*
(dialogue to **dialogue or dialog)**

British to *American*
 -our to *-or*
colour – *color*
favourite – *favorite*
honour – *honor*
behaviour – *behavior*
neighbour – *neighbor*
flavour – *flavor*
humour – *humor*
labour – *labor*
odour – *odor*
rumour – *rumor*
saviour – *savior*
demeanour – *demeanor*
harbour – *harbor*
savoury – *savory*
splendour – splendor
glamour – *glamor* or *glamour*

Be careful, American spelling still has:
our, your, hour, four, flour, dour, sour, tour, scour, detour,
devour, contour, pour, velour

British to *American*
-re to -er
centre – *center*
metre – *meter*
centimetre – *centimeter*
fibre – *fiber*
litre – *liter*
sombre – *somber*
theatre – *theater* and *theatre*

These words are still spelled with –**re** in American: *acre, massacre, lucre, mediocre, ogre.*

British to *American*
-ise to -ize

According to the *Oxford Dictionary*, both endings are correct in British English but only one way in American. Canadians usually use -**ize**. They recommend you choose one style and stick to it within a piece of writing. The *Oxford Dictionary* uses the –**ize** ending on their website, probably because the -**ize** ending is older and closer to its Greek roots. But –**ise** is more widely used.

British English -ise or ize	American English -ize
realise or realize	realize
apologise or apologize	apologize
organise or organize	organize
recognise or recognize	recognise or recognize
finalise or finalize	finalize

CAREFUL, a few words must only be spelled with –**ise**: *advertise, advise, chastise, compromise, despise, devise, disguise, excise, exercise, improvise, promise.*

No doubling of the final 'l'
This applies to words of more than one syllable ending in 'l' when adding a vowel suffix/ending.

British: cancel - cancelling, cancelled, cancellation
American: cancel - canceling, canceled, cancelation

British: marvel - marvellous, marvelled, marvelling
American: marvel - marvelous, marveled, marveling

British: travel - travelling, travelled, traveller
American: travel – traveling, traveled, traveler

British: jewel - jewellery, jeweller
American: jewel - jewelry, jeweler

British – *American*
modelled/modelling – *modeled/modeling*
quarelled/quarelling – *quarreled/quarreling*
counsellor – *counselor*
equalled – *equaled*
fuelling/fuelled – *fueling/fueled*
grovelled/grovelling – *groveled/groveling*
woollen – *woolen*

This also applies to a few American words when the stress falls on a syllable other than the first.

conTROL   paTROL
controlled   *patrolled*
controlling   *patrolling*
annulled, expelled, extolled

Be careful with these words:
British English: enrol - *enrolling, enrolled*
American English: *enroll* ends in double 'l', so *enrolling, enrolled.*

Both American and British agree not to double the end 'l' in parallel - *parallels, paralleling, paralleled.*

But be careful with these words:

British single 'l' – American double 'l'

appal – appall

distil – distill

enrol – enroll

enthral – enthrall

fulfil – fulfill

instil – instill

skilful – skillful

wilful – willful

Some spelling differs between American and British words. In most cases, American words have fewer letters.

***American* – British**

licorice – liquorice

program – programme but computer program

maneuve – manoeuvre

sulfur – sulphur

naught – nought

skeptic – sceptic

vial – phial

Exercise
Do you know the British spellings of these American spellings?

write a check -

cozy -

donut -

roadside curb -

mustache -

omelet -

pajamas -

car tire -

gray -

Exercise Answers

Am - *write a check*
Br - cheque

Am - *cozy*
Br - cosy

Am - *donut*
Br - doughnut

Am - *roadside curb*
Br - kerb

Am - *mustache*
Br - moustache

Am - *omelet*
Br - omelette

Am - *pajamas*
Br - pyjamas

Am - *tire*
Br - tyre

Am - *gray*
Br - grey

American or British?

The following words are useful to know so we can understand
each other on holidays/vacations, working in/going to
restaurants, watching each other's films and TV shows, etc.

Clothes

American	British
pants	trousers
underwear / panties	pants / knickers / underwear
sneakers	trainers
diaper	nappy
sweater	jumper / sweater / pullover
turtle neck	polo neck
gym shoes	plimsolls / plimsoles

Food

American	British
zucchini	courgette
eggplant	aubergine
cookie	biscuit
candy	sweets
jelly	jam
jello	jelly
potato chips	crisps
fries/French fries	chips
arugula	rocket
cilantro	coriander
takeout	takeaway
Plus in restaurants:	
check	bill
napkin	serviette

American	British
flashlight	torch
Band-Aid	plaster
fall	autumn
national holiday	bank holiday
elevator	lift
stand in line	queue
There's a line	There's a queue
It's spoiled	It's gone off
ladybug	ladybird
trash can	dustbin/rubbish bin/bin
closet	wardrobe
sidewalk	pavement
parking lot	car park
gas/gasoline	petrol
fire truck	fire engine
freeway	motorway
vacation	holiday
math	maths

Key Spelling Rules

People say spelling is chaotic - it's not. It's complicated, yes, but there are regularities with it and it can be learnt, and one way is through learning spelling rules, which adds another layer to your spelling knowledge.

Knowing spelling rules, and the exceptions to the rules, is a great strategy to help you understand why spelling is the way it is and helps you spell. That's why we've looked at some rules throughout the book, especially in the sections on phonics and suffixes.

Some people think if they learn a spelling rule, they'll be able to spell. Unfortunately, the trouble with rules is you have to remember the rule, and which words work with the rule and the words that don't! But some people like learning rules and get a buzz out of finding out how to use them.

So even if you forget the rule, maybe you'll remember the spelling pattern, and at least you hopefully will know why a spelling is the way it is.

A health warning: rules are complicated to explain, and there are many exceptions. "Good" spellers, who appear to understand spelling rules and principles, often apply other strategies. They may have good visual memories, which recognize differences in word construction. They may have learnt strategies (mnemonics or syllable counting) that have given them an understanding of how words behave, so they begin to "know" when spellings are wrong.
Basic Skills Agency: *Starter Pack*

This section is a brief look at five key rules. For an in-depth look at spelling rules, check out my *Spelling Rules Workbook – a step-by-step guide to the rules of English spelling*, available on my website and Amazon.

Top Five Spelling Rules

Rule 1. Adding –ly to words – 7 rules

1. Add -ly to whole words ending in a consonant.

slow + ly = *slowly*   quick + ly = *quickly*

apparent + ly = *apparently*   care + less + ly = *carelessly*

2. Add -ly to words ending in 'l' (this makes double 'l')

real + ly = *really*   total + ly = *totally*

faithful + ly = *faithfully* final + ly = *finally*

3. Add -ly to words ending in –ful (this makes double 'l')

careful + ly = *carefully*   hopeful + ly = *hopefully*

beautiful + ly = *beautifully*   *usefully, faithfully,*

4. We usually keep the 'e'.

love + ly = *lovely*   complete + ly = *completely*

immediate + ly = *immediately*   definite + ly = *definitely*

The big exception to this is often misspelled (*truly*)

truly = true + ly ➔ drop the 'e' = *truly*

Also, due + ly = *duly*   whole + ly = *wholly*

5. Change the 'e' to 'y' in words ending in -ble, -tle, -ple...

simple ➔ *simply*   possible ➔ *possibly*

subtle ➔ *subtly*   probable ➔ *probably*

6. Change the end 'y' to 'i' in words of more than one syllable.

happy + ly = happily   crazy ➔ crazily   easy ➔ easily

But this doesn't apply to one syllable words: *shyly, slyly, coyly.* But exceptions are: day ➔ *daily*   gay ➔ *gaily*

7. We add –ally to words ending in –ic.

basic + ally = *basically*   ecstatic + ally = *ecstatically*

comically, cynically, ethically, logically, magically, medically, musically

A big exception is *publicly* = public + ly

If a word ends in –al just add ly.
incidental ➔ *incidentally*   musical ➔ *musically*

Look at these patterns:
incident – incidental – incidentally,
music – musical – musically
comic – comical – comically, magic – magical – magically...

Also, you can add –ly to those –ous words we saw earlier:
famous – *famously,* anxious – *anxiously, viciously,*
dangerously, nervously, cautiously, enormously, seriously...

Rule 2. Drop the 'e' rule

Drop the 'e' with –ing
come + ing = *coming*   write + ing = *writing*
complete + ing = *completing*   manage + ing = managing
argue + ing = *arguing*   congratulate - *congratulating*
having, celebrating, changing, achieving, believing, arguing...

But not with words ending in –ee or –oe.
free - *freeing, seeing, foreseeing,* agreeing, guaranteeing,
kneeing, canoe – *canoeing,* hoeing, shoeing, tiptoeing

Or keep the 'e' if it changes the word to another meaning
dye – *dyeing* (not dying), singe – *singeing* (not singing),
whingeing

Drop the 'e' with –able/–ible
achieve + able = *achievable*   believe + able = *believable*
response + ible = *responsible*   sense + ible = *sensible*
writable, arguable, believable, recognisable/recognizable,
collapsible, excusable, pleasurable...

We keep the 'e' with words ending in soft 'c' or 'g' to maintain the soft 'c' and 'g' sounds
notice + able = *noticeable*   manage - *manageable*
knowledge + able = *knowledgeable* change - *changeable*
marriage – *marriageable*   service – *serviceable*

If the word has a hard "g" and "c" sound, we use –able: *navigable, delegable, despicable amicable, applicable, impeccable...*

Some spellings can keep or drop the 'e': *likeable/likable, useable/usable, sizeable/sizable*

Keep the 'e' with words ending in double 'e': *foreseeable, unforeseeable, agreeable*

Drop the 'e' with other vowel suffixes
continue – *continuous, continued, continuator, continuing*
nerve – *nervous, nervy*
hesitate – *hesitant, hesitation, hesitating, hesitancy*
separate – *separation, separating, separable, inseparable*

-ation: adore – *adoration*, sense – *sensation*, prepare – *preparation*, admire - *admiration*

Careful, we drop the 'e' with a consonant suffix in these words:
argue – *argument*   awe – *awful* (but *awesome*)
due – *duly*   true – *truly*   whole - *wholly*

Rule 3. (Revision) 'y' to 'i' rule
Change the end 'y' to 'i' when adding suffixes (except –ing/ -ible) and 'y' to 'ies' for plurals and third person he/she/ it.

happy ➜ *happiness, happily, happier, happiest*
tidy ➜ *tidier, tidies, tidied, tidiest, tidily, tidiness*
lonely ➜ *loneliness, lonelier, loneliest*
busy ➜ *busier, busiest, busily, business*
temporary ➜ *temporarily, temporariness*
angry ➜ *angrily, angrier, angriest*
marry ➜ *married, marries, marriage, marriageable*
beauty ➜ *beautiful, beauties, beautician, beautify*
justify ➜ *justified, justifies, justifiable, justification*
accessory ➜ *accessories, accessorize/accessorise*
luxury ➜ *luxuries, luxurious luxuriate, luxuriant, luxuriated*

Rule 4. **1:1:1 doubling up rule** or the twinning rule
put - putting, big - bigger, biggest, quiz - quizzes

When a word has 1 syllable + 1 vowel next to 1 consonant, we double up the final consonant with a <u>vowel suffix</u>:

sit – *sitter, sitting,* big – *bigger, biggest,* tap - *tapping, tapped*
hot – *hotter, hottest, hottie*
sad – *sadder, sadden, saddened, saddest*
blur – *blurring, blurred, blurry*
shop – *shopper, shopping, shopped*
fat - *fatten, fattening, fatter, fattest, fatty*
swim – *swimmer, swimming, swimmingly*
quiz – *quizzes, quizzed, quizzing, quizzer, quizzical*
whiz – *whizzes, whizzed, whizzing, whizzer*

> Remember to only double up with vowel suffixes. Compare these: *dropper/droplet, inner/inward, sunny/sunless hottest/hotly, goddess/godly, shipping/shipment redden/redness, swimmer/swims, strappy/strapless*

The 1:1:1 doubling up rule happens in longer words when the stress is on the final syllable:
begin "beGIN" - *beginner, beginning*
defer "deFER" – *defer, deferred, deferring* (not deference)
refer "reFER" - *referring, referred, referral*
(not *reference* "REFerence", referendum)
prefer – *preferred, preferring*
(not *preferable, preference,* preferential)
occur "ocCUR" - *occurring, occurred, occurrence* "ocCURrence"
equip – *equipped, equipper, equipping* (but *equipment* - consonant suffix)
commit – *committed, committing, committable, committee*
forget – *forgetting, forgettable, forgotten*

We never double up *w, x, y* or *c.*

Rule 5. (Revision) Adding -es to words

Add -es to words ending in -s, -ss, -z -ch -sh –x.

bus → *buses*   business → *businesses*
wash → *washes*   watch → *watches*
box → *boxes*   waitress → *waitresses*
waltz → *waltzes*
 quiz → *quizzes* (1:1:1 doubling up rule too)
riches, beaches, stretches, foxes, varnishes, witnesses, flushes

A few useful little rules

-c to -ck
When adding vowel suffixes (–ing, -ed, -er or –y) to words ending in –ic, we must add 'k' to keep the hard "c" sound:
picnic – *picnicking, picnicked, picnicker*
panic – *panicked, panicking, panicky*
traffic – *trafficking, trafficked*
mimic – *mimicking, mimicked* (but not *mimicry*)

Double letters in compound words
Compound words are words that are made up of two words. Notice the double letters in these words.
ear + ring = *earring*   book + keeper = *bookkeeper*
with + hold = *withhold*   *room + mate = roommate*
hitchhike, newsstand, barroom, knickknack...

Two exceptions are *pastime* and *wherever*.
We actually say "pas time" = to pass time.

In British English, we drop the 'u' in –our words with –ary, -ous, -ist, -ise/-ize, making it the same as the American spelling.

British – BrE/AmE
honour – *hon*o*rary*   labour – *laborious*
humour – *humorous, humorist*   amour – *amorous*
rigour – *rigorous, rigorist*   vigour – *vigorous*
glamour – *glamorous, glamorise/glamorize*

Drop 'u' in the -ous when adding -sity
(the pronunciation helps and also breaks into syllables well)

generous – *generosity*   curious – *curiosity*

monstrous – *monstrosity*   fabulous – *fabulosity*

pompous – *pomposity*   virtuous – *virtuosity*

Change the -cious to -city
(notice the sound changes from "sh" to "s")

fero**cious** - *fero**city***

atrocious - *atrocity*

precocious – *precocity*

pugnacious – *pugnacity*

An understanding of spelling rules helps you discover more rules and riddles for yourself. This fuels interest, engagement and thinking skills.
Sally Raymond: *Spelling Rules, Riddles and Remedies*

Exercise. Use your knowledge of these spelling rules, or visual memory, to decide which is correct.

1. a. mooddy   b. moody

2. a. bloodiest   b. bloodyest

3. a. fraudulent   b. frauddulent

4. a. foxxy   b. foxy

5. a. boxes   b. boxs

6. a. reference   b. referrence

7. a. iffy   b. ify

8. a. truly   b. truely

9. a. panicing   b. panicking

10. a. watchs   b. watches

12. a. forgoten   b. forgotten

Exercise Answers

1. a. mooddy   **b. moody**

2. **a. bloodiest**   b. bloodyest

3. **a. fraudulent**   b. frauddulent

4. a. foxxy   **b. foxy**

5. **a. boxes**   b. boxs

6. **a. reference**   b. referrence

7. **a. iffy**   b. ify

8. **a. truly**   b. truely

9. a. panicing   **b. panicking**

10. a. watchs   **b. watches**

12. a. forgoten   **b. forgotten**

Spelling Rules and Suffixes Revision Exercise

word	root word	suffix(es)	spelling rule(s)
happiness	happy	ness	change y to i
wishes			
beginning			
slowly			
generosity			
forgotten			
busiest			
responsible			
finally			
picnicking			
changeable			
arguing			
hopefully			
beautician			

Exercise Answers.

word	root word	suffix(es)	spelling rule(s)
happiness	happy	ness	change **y** to **i**
wishes	wish	es	add **es** to **sh**
beginning	begin	ing	double up rule
slowly	slow	ly	add **ly**
generosity	generous	-ity /-sity	drop the **u**
forgotten	forgot	en	double up rule
busiest	busy	est	change **y** to **i**
responsible	response	-ible	drop the **e**
finally	final	ly	add **ly**
picnicking	picnic	ing	add **k** to **c**
changeable	change	able	keep the **e** to keep the soft **g** sound
arguing	argue	ing	drop the **e**
hopefully	hope	ful + ly	add **ful** + **ly**
beautician	beauty	cian	change **y** to **i**

Job Application Words

+ revision of some words

We all know how important it is to spell perfectly on application forms, and on your CV (curriculum vitae) (BrE) / résumé (AmE).

If you don't know, or are unsure of a spelling, then use a dictionary or online dictionary - this is an important strategy. When we don't use 'big', 'formal' words all the time, we tend to forget how to spell them, so please, please, please use a dictionary.

Self-Assessment Exercise

Do you know how to spell the important words below?
Can you use any spelling strategies to help?

1. a. referrence   b. reference   c. referance

2. a. sucessful   b. succesfull   c. successful

3. a. beginner   b. beginer   c. begginner

4. a. tommorrow   b. tomorrow   c. tommorow

5. a. achievable   b. achieveable   c. acheivable

6. a. responsibilitys   b. responsibilties   c. responsibilities

7. a. preference   b. preferrence   c. prefference

8. a. particulary   b. particulalary   c. particularly

9. a. commumicater   b. communicator   c. comunnicator

10. a. experiance   b. experience   c. experrience

11. a. applying   b. appliing   c. aplying

12. a. applycation   b. aplication   c. application

Exercise Answers

1. a. referrence   **b. reference**   c. referance

2. a. sucessful   b. succesfull   **c. successful**

3. **a. beginner**   b. beginer   c. begginner

4. a. tommorrow   **b. tomorrow**   c. tommorow

5. **a. achievable**   b. achieveable   c. acheivable

6. a. responsibilitys   b. responsibilties   **c. responsibilities**

7. **a. preference**   b. preferrence   c. prefference

8. a. particulary   b. particulalary   **c. particularly**

9. a. commumicater   **b. communicator**   c. comunnicator

10. a. experiance   **b. experience**   c. experrience

11. **a. applied**   b. applyed   c. aplied

12. a. applycation   b. aplication   **c. application**

My responsibilities included liaising with managers and communicating with customer services.

Applicants should demonstrate a familiarity with housing regulations.

I would like to apply for the position of Environmental Liaison Officer.

I have five years' experience as an office manager.

apply
applying

Remember to change the 'y' to 'i' with suffixes except –ing and -ish
applied
application ("ap pli ca tion" – syllable breakdown)
applicable ("ap pli ca ble")

Remember the "**happy**" words.
*I was **happy** to **apply** and **I** filled in an **application** with all the **applicable** information.*

success   double 'c' and double 's'
Double Congratulations on your Super Success.
Constant Congratulations on your Super Success.
successful = success + ful = *successful*
successfully = success + ful + ly = *successfully*

succeed double 'c' and double 'e'
Only 3 words end in –**ceed**: *exceed, succeed, proceed.*

I succeeded in exceeding their expectations and will now proceed exceedingly quickly and successfully.

achieve "i before e except after c" rule applies here
achieved
achieving (drop the 'e' with –ing)
achievable (drop the 'e' with –able)
achievement, achievements (keep the 'e')
It gave me a great sense of achievement to achieve top marks in the test.

Think of some memory tricks and sentences for the following words.

refer
referring, referred, referral, referrer (doubling up rule)
reference, referee, referendum (no double 'r'. Notice all the e's)

liaise Notice those i's
liaison (drop the 'e')   use the first letters to make up a saying: *Live in an igloo, son*
liaising (drop the 'e')

communicate We communicate through Mass Media.
communicator
communication

experience Notice all the e's and i in the middle "ex pe ri ence".
experienced

manage
managing (drop the 'e' with –ing)
managed
manager
management (manage + ment)
manageable (keep the 'e' to keep the 'g' soft)

environment (don't forget the "iron")

committee Many Meetings are Terribly Tedious.

colleague "col league"

questio<u>nn</u>aire (double n) question + naire

Questionnaire and *legionnaire* are borrowed from French.

Be careful, **single n** in *billionaire, extraordinaire, millionaire, Apollinaire, commissionaire, concessionaire...*

entrepreneur Can you see all those e's? **entrepreneur** entre pre neur

particular (syllable breakdown "par tic u lar")

particular + ly = **particularly**

---

begin
beginning (1:1:1 doubling up rule)
beginnings
beginner

---

familiar I'm *familiar* with that *peculiar* **liar**.
familiarise / familiarize
familiarity "fa mil i a ri ty"

---

tomorrow "Good **morrow**" was the old way of saying good day.
to + morrow = tomorrow
tomorrow/borrow/sorrow/furrow/marrow/arrow/sparrow

The single word most commonly misspelled is **"responsibility"**, a worrying error considering how many people use it to flag up their attractions to potential employers. (telegraph.co.uk)
responsible
responsibility (notice all the i's)
responsibility = *responsible* - drop the 'le' and add –ility
Break it into syllables: re/spon/sib/il/i/ty or re/spon/si/bil/ity

(plural) **responsibilities** (notice all the i's)   the end 'y' becomes 'ies'

Responsibility sounds like and has the same –**ility** pattern as these words. (This naturally breaks into syllables so helps with the spelling.)
ability, agility, civility, docility, utility, futility, facility, fertility, stability, liability, hostility, versatility, mobility, tranquility, nobility, humility, fragility...

Letter endings

I look forward to hearing from you.
hearing – ear, hear, hearing

for + ward = *forward*
straightforward, henceforward

-ward(s) = direction: *forward (towards the future), towards, onward, upward, backward, sideward, homeward, eastward, westward...*

Yours sincerely, (use when you know their name: Dear Jane Smith, Dear Miss Smith.)
since + rely = sincerely (**since** I **since**rely rely on you)
(Also in AmE – Sincerely yours)

Yours sincerely, Joanne
Sincerely yours, Joanne

Yours faithfully (use when you don't know name and using Dear Sir/Madam)
faith + ful + l y = faithfully

Now write a personal statement about your experience, job responsibilities, goals and achievements.

Or just write some sentences with these job application words.

Revision Exercise

Which are correct? Use your strategies to help. If you're not sure, then go back and check.

1. a. unneccesary   b. unnecessary   c. unecessary

2. a. embarrasing   b. embarrassing   c. embarassing

3. a. tomorow   b. tommorrow   c. tomorrow

4. a. signifecant   b. significent   c. significant

5. a. Wednsday   b. Wenesday   c. Wednesday

6. 40 = a. fourty   b. fourrty   c. forty

7. 9th = a. nineth   b. ninth   c. nineneth

8. a. business   b. bussiness   c. businness

9. a. occasionally   b. ocasionally   c. occasionaly

10. a. questionaire   b. questionnaire   c. questionnare

11. a. referrence   b. referance   c. reference

12. a. experience   b. experiance   c. expearience

13. a. truely   b. truly   c. truley

14. a. responsibilities   b. responsabilities   c. responsibilties

15. a. acheivements   b. achievmrnts   c. achievements

16. a. sincerley   b. sincerely   c. sincearly

247

Revision Exercise Answers

1. a. unneccesary   **b. unnecessary**   c. unecessary

2. a. embarrasing   **b. embarrassing**   c. embarassing

3. a. tomorow   b. tommorrow   **c. tomorrow**

4. a. signifecant   b. significent   **c. significant**

5. a. Wednsday   b. Wenesday   **c. Wednesday**

6. 40 = a. fourty   b. fourrty   **c. forty**

7. 9th = a. nineth   **b. ninth**   c. nineneth

8. **a. business**   b. bussiness   c. businness

9. **a. occasionally**   b. ocasionally   c. occasionaly

10. a. questionaire   **b. questionnaire**   c. questionnare

11. a. referrence   b. referance   **c. reference**

12. **a. experience**   b. experiance   c. expearience

13. a. truely   **b. truly**   c. truley

14. **a. responsibilities**   b. responsabilities   c. responsibilties

15. a. acheivements   b. achievments   **c. achievements**

16. a. sincerley   **b. sincerely**   c. sincearly

Your Spelling Stories

You're not alone in wanting help with spelling. I get emails every day from native speakers from the UK, USA, Australia, Canada, etc. who feel let down by their education. These people are in their thirties to sixties. I even get people in college/high school who struggle with their spelling, or people who are home schooling their kids and need help.

Now more than ever, we need to spell and write with confidence. We rely on emails and social media to stay in touch with our friends and colleagues, to feel part of society, to belong to a social group. This need, or pressure, to be "social" involves writing, but maybe because of this, more people are sharing videos and "cute" pictures rather than writing how they feel because they don't want to show themselves up with their spelling.

I can see how some people struggle with spelling when they write comments or Facebook updates, and it's painful to see. I don't judge these people, but others will. Part of the problem is people don't proofread their words. Another stupid thing is predictive text. I don't know how many times I've been caught out by typing too quickly and missed or transposed a letter, and the predictive text has written something completely different. So always, always proofread the tiniest email, comment, etc.

In this section are some of the emails I've received from around the world. When necessary, I've proofread and corrected typos and punctuation to make it easier to read. But the stories are all in their own words and feelings.

> I'm 57, a grandma, and work online. I lost jobs over my spelling and was so depressed. Spelling has always held me back in life but not anymore. I feel differently about spelling now because I understand it better. I can see a way forward. Alison, UK

I work in my local hospital on a maternity unit - we're called maternity support workers. We need to write in the mother's notes but I've always shied away from writing in them because of my spelling and my handwriting - it's so embarrassing. Anyway, since doing your course, I've noticed my handwriting and spelling have improved. I can't explain how much this means to me and to say thank you. The confidence I have, I feel like I'm walking on air. And if you would have told me I would be writing this email this time last week, I would have said no way. Annette, UK

I was brought up in the fifties and I am naturally left-handed, but was made to write with my right hand as left-handers are backward! So from the age of five to ten, I refused to write. That changed when I was hit (on my right hand) by Sister Angela with the edge of the ruler in front of the whole class and told to return to my desk and write! Which I did, but this time, I could only use my left hand and was left alone to do so!!! However, that experience has not left me, or being tagged as backward!!! E. G. USA

I've improved so much in my spelling, and I'm less embarrassed and afraid to write on paper or on the computer than I was before I started these lessons. It's a worthwhile journey for me.

When I was in primary school, I tried using vocabulary in my composition in class and, as you can imagine, I got all the spellings wrong for all the vocabulary I tried to use. My teacher read the composition and embarrassed me so much that I vowed never to learn anymore vocabulary, well, until I came across your website and learned all the tricks. Now I can use and learn new words and spell the tricky ones. Sherry, UK.

Thank you so much for all your lessons. I have been trying to spell, it's not easy. I'm 52 and do lots of things helping others but when it comes to writing names and address, I just seize up. Pauline, Ireland

My experience at school was awful, the worst time of my life. Nothing made any sense to me, the letters just kept moving around on the paper. The headmaster told my parents that I was mentally abnormal, said they couldn't teach me anything. I left school unable to read or write.

At 15, I went straight into factory work. I managed to work for 24 years. I taught myself to read and write a little but my spelling is not very good. Thanks to you I'm getting better and more confident. David.

The biggest reason that I didn't go to school in the first and second grades was because of "Spelling Bees". I was just too embarrassed to attend class, so I just told everyone that I was sick so they would keep me home. Although I'm sure that Spelling Bees are a very useful tool for teachers, I was never so embarrassed in my life.

To this day, I feel very sorry for children that are now going through what I had to when I was young. Can you imagine trying to say something with everyone staring at just you and not knowing what to say? I hated school because of Spelling Bees, along with having to get up in front of the class: too much of being put on display, in my book. HK, USA

I don't know how I found you on the internet, but am so pleased I did. I was looking for a basic English course at my local college (well, spelling really), just a refresher course. You have saved me the embarrassment of attending college by sending me great work I can do at home. I love doing the spelling tests, etc. and with so much to choose from, I feel I have improved in such a short time. The spelling patterns, rules, words within words - why did I never see that? I am so grateful to you for your help. Regards, Christine, UK

I am 57 years old and just watched the first video session with "able". Wish I had you as my English teacher back in my primary years. This is the first time I actually enjoyed learning to spell. Your method of teaching will also help my little 6-year-old grandson to learn to spell. Thank you. Regards Jill, UK

I'm 44 years old and I've always had a problem with spelling. I work in an organization where I need to communicate in English. Sometimes, I have to stand up in meetings and write on a whiteboard. You can imagine how difficult it is if you have bad spelling. However, now I use spelling strategies to help and I feel much better. Y, Qatar

I'm sixty years old and never really liked spelling when I was at school. I started a website a few years ago, which helped me somewhat with my spelling, but I no longer have it.

I work for a big supermarket and have just started on security so need to be able to spell. I think I tend to spell words the way they sound. So I think it's a matter of going through and trying to memorise the spelling patterns and use memory tricks. Trev, UK

I'm doing my GCSE maths and English level 2 – that will help me get into my career. Hope to meet you in the future. You're much better than MPs and people that are in charge of education.

In my opinion, I think many people run away from school because they don't teach something that makes sense. People won't spend hours practising something but your course is easy to understand and straightforward. Adan, London

My spelling demons have been haunting me for years, but even more recently because I have to teach and create presentations at a professional level. In my case, I lost out on the early years of school because of eye troubles and never really got to catch up. Whilst not officially tested, I am convinced that I suffer with dyslexia. You can imagine the embarrassment and frustration I try to hide on a daily basis. Anyway, I am sure that my story is not dissimilar to so many others and now at 41 years old, I am finally getting the help and support I need.

Now that I understand that there is a logic to spelling, it excites me to learn patterns and word sums, etc. and the memory tricks are great too - here's one of mine! "It's only *visible* with two eyes (i's)."

Even after a few days of using the strategies, my spelling has measurably improved and I am starting to enjoy writing for the first time in my life. Credit where credit is due. Matt, Ireland

It has been a while but since we last talked I have published two papers and been massively involved in a university-related project. So my time is at a premium these days. I would like to tell you that my spelling really has improved but more importantly is my confidence. Often now I question words that I never would have before. When this happens, I visit the online Oxford Dictionary which has become like a friend. Kindest regards, Matt, Ireland

I just want to be good at English so I can do more things. I have an idea for writing books but am unable to put it down because of my problems. After listening to your voice on your videos, I was surprised how happy I was. Chris, UK.

My Spelling Experience by Darren Johnson, UK

School should be the best times of our lives, that's what people say, so why did so many of us get let down by school?

I started infant school in the early 70s and finished secondary school in 1982, and it still hurts me to this day how let down I feel with my schooling, and teachers who were happy with their day's work by not bothering. My history teacher used to say, "if you don't want to learn, I'll sign you in and you can go home until the next class".

It's the most precious time in our lives because it sets us up for the rest of our lives, and yes, it set a lot of us up on the scrap heap!

I was allowed to leave school at fourteen because my mum and dad split up and I moved away with my mum and two brothers. So I missed the last two years and didn't take any exams - how could they have allowed this?

I can remember being in remedial English with only six of us there. When asked to read a book, I would say I can't because the words were moving - was this fear or just trying to hide, or dyslexia? I feel so hurt by my schooling. Or did this set me up in life to work with my hands, which I've been lucky enough to do?

Enough of me moaning. 25 years after leaving school, I felt I owed it to myself to stop hiding from spelling and try and do something about it. I've been working really hard the last eight years to try and improve. I feel I've come a long way but I know I have at least another five years to get to where I want to be.

It's amazing - in the last eight years I've taken my Level 1 and 2 English and Maths exams and passed. This is something you should pass when you're 16 years old - I feel a fool but also very proud.

So now I'm 50 this year and I want to get more into management but need to spell a lot better. Lucky for me, we all have spell- check on our phones and computers. But my spelling was so bad that my computer couldn't even help me.

After trying so many different ways to spell, I've learnt the only way that works for me is writing a word down twenty times a day for two weeks. After a few months, you start to see you only need to add a few letters and you have a new word. So you start to learn that you don't need to learn a 8 or 9 letter word - you just need to add a few letters to the 4 or 6 letter word you've learnt.

I now find it really easy to spell *friend* but after reading a few books, I see that lots of people find this hard. I just look at the "*end*" on the end and 'i' before 'e' so all I need to know is "fr". I could never spell *Chris* but all I do is think "is" on the end and then all I need now is "Chr".

For years, when spelling a person's name like *Brian,* I would put Brain, but little tips like just put *Ian* on the end just like *Julian.*

I was never taught how to break words down as a kid, let alone spelling strategies, rules, prefixes and suffixes. Now I'm reading shop fronts, and vans with writing on and noticing lots of words with words in them. It's amazing how it's slowly coming together.

The happy ending! I'm a director of a construction company. We work for a lot of VIPs. We're very lucky with work. We're always turning it away. So as you can see I've done very well. I'm a Chartered Builder or a Chartered Construction Manager. I have a level 7 in Site Management plus level 6 and 3, and many more different NVQS. So I have letters after my name when I need to use them for work!

Do you have a spelling story? Let me know at:
info@howtospell.co.uk

Book & Website Recommendations

Murray Suid: *Demonic Mnemonics* (Fearon)

Shireen Shuster: *Spelling Essentials* (Longman)

Joy Pollock: *Signposts to Spelling* (Blessings)

Joanne Rudling: *Spelling Rules Workbook* (How to Spell Publishing)

Joanne Rudling: *The Reasons Why English Spelling is so Weird and Wonderful* (How to Spell Publishing)

Joanne Rudling: *How to Spell the 20 Most Commonly Misspelled Words Workbook And Journal* (How to Spell Publishing)

Joanne Rudling: *Punctuation Guide & Workbook* (How to Spell Publishing)

Gena K. Gorrell: *"Say What?"* (Tundra Books)

David Crystal: *Words Words Words* (Oxford)

David Crystal: *The Stories of English* (Penguin)

Larry Beason: *Eyes before Ease* (McGraw-Hill)

Anne Betteridge: *Adult Learners' Guide to Spelling* (Chambers)

Catherine Taylor: *A Useful Spelling Handbook for Adults* (Olympia)

G. Terry Page: *The Book of Spelling Rules* (Wordsworth Reference)

Meryl Wilkins: *Improve our Spelling in English* (NIACE)

Pacquita Boston: *The Inside Story of Spelling*

Websites

www.howtospell.co.uk

www.bbc.co.uk/skillswise

www.beatingdyslexia.com

www.grammar-monster.com

www.curious.com/howtospell

Online Dictionaries with pronunciation and example sentences

www.oxforddictionaries.com - British & American

www.macmillandictionary.com - British & American

http://dictionary.cambridge.org - British & American

www.merriam-webster.com - American

For Teachers

Johanna Stirling: *Teaching Spelling to English Language Learners* (her blog - http://thespellingblog.blogspot.co.uk)

Sally Raymond: *Spelling Rules, Riddles and Remedies* (Routledge)

Bear, Invernizzi, Templeton, Johnston: *Words Their Way* (Pearson)

Lyn Stone: *Spelling For Life* (Routledge)

Spelling Pack (Basic Skills Agency)

The Starter Pack (Basic Skills Agency)

Edward Carney: *English Spelling* (Routledge)

Sue Abell: *Helping Adults to Spell* (ALBSU)

Cynthia. Klein: *Learning to Spell – or Spelling to Learn* (ALBSU)

Cynthia Klein: *Unscrambling Spelling*

D.W. Cummings: *American English Spelling* (John Hopkins)

David Crystal: *Spell it Out* (Profile Books)

Research Paper: Kelly, Soundranayagam, Grief: *Teaching and learning writing: a review of research and practice.* June 2004. (National Research and Development Centre for adult literacy and numeracy.)

About the Author

Joanne Rudling is a freelance lecturer, teacher trainer, and owner of www.howtospell.co.uk.

She's taught spelling, literacy and writing for 20 years in various organizations including: the City of Westminster College, Bournemouth FE College, Dorset Adult Education, Bournemouth University, and Bournemouth Film School.

Joanne has developed and taught on literacy projects for the Pre-Volunteer Programme for the Olympics, and the RNIB (Royal National Institute for the Blind).

She also edits closed captions/subtitles from American spellings to British for Amazon.com TV drama division.

Other books by Joanne on Amazon, & howtospell.co.uk
Spelling Rules Workbook – a step-by-step guide to the rules of English spelling (hard copy and ebook)
How to Spell the 20 Most Commonly Misspelled Words (hard copy)
QTS Spelling Strategies to Help You Pass the Literacy Skills Spelling Test (hard copy and ebook)
Punctuation Guide and Workbook (hard copy and ebook)
The Reasons Why English Spelling is so Weird and Wonderful (ebook)

Online courses (check them out on howtospell.co.uk)
Spelling Rules, Patterns and Strategies Masterclass
Homophones Masterclass

Online video courses on curious.com/howtospell
Rules of English Spelling
Beginner's Guide to English Punctuation
ESL Spelling Strategies

~~~